LEVEL UP YOUR HAPPINESS

How to
USE YOUR STRENGTHS
to
THRIVE IN YOUR LIFE

MICHAEL C. OSTER

Copyright © 2024 by Michael C. Oster.

All rights reserved. This book or any portion thereof may not be reproduced or used in any manner whatsoever without the express written permission of the publisher except for the use of brief quotations in a book review.

The Level Up Method™ is a trademark of Michael C. Oster.

The 24 names of Character Strengths are trademarks of the VIA Institute; the 34 theme names of CliftonStrengths® are trademarks of Gallup, Inc. All rights reserved.

The non-VIA and the non-Gallup information presented here has not been approved and is not sanctioned or endorsed by VIA or Gallup in any way. Opinions, views, and interpretations of strengths are solely the beliefs of Michael C. Oster.

Publishing Services provided by Paper Raven Books

Printed in the United States of America

Library of Congress Control Number: 2024921945

Paperback ISBN: 978-1-7341191-5-2
Hardback ISBN: 978-1-7341191-4-5
eBook ISBN: 978-1-7341191-3-8

Be yourself. Everyone else is taken.

– OSCAR WILDE

CONTENTS

Preface   1
Introduction: Life by the Inch   3
Chapter 1: The Level Up Method   13

PART I

Your Strengths   19
Chapter 2: Thinking   35
Chapter 3: Connecting   45
Chapter 4: Enabling   55
Chapter 5: Performing   65
Chapter 6: Believing   79

PART II

The Competencies   87
Chapter 7: Planning   99
Chapter 8: Changing   115
Chapter 9: Collaborating   143
Chapter 10: Accomplishing   173
Chapter 11: Improving   187

PART III

The Next Version of You 207
Chapter 12: Your Personal Development Plan 211

About the Author 219
Appendix 221
Index 227

PREFACE

Thank you for reading this new edition of *Level Up*.

The first one, in 2020, was for members of teams in organizations. In its blue cover, *Level Up: How to Use Your Unique Strengths to Improve Your Competencies and Reach Your Goals* introduced the Level Up Method, a new technique to engage our most potent strengths to efficiently achieve results when working with others.

This new edition is for everyone who wishes to elevate their happiness and thrive in their life.

Here you will learn a new way to use your natural strengths to think and do the things which will help you live a happier more fulfilling life. Being happy, living well and doing well, is a fine way to live our lives How much happiness we have is a good indicator of how we are living up to our potential.

HOW TO READ THIS BOOK

If you love a long lavish buffet with many appealing items, you may enjoy reading the book cover to cover. For you, considering and choosing the items to include in your meal is an adventure.

If you prefer assembling your own menu, feel free to read more selectively. Spend your time and your imagination exploring the strengths that feel most like yours and the specific competencies you would like to improve.

Select whichever approach gives you the most pleasure. Read all the passages or spend your time with the ones that resonate most with you. Your choice.

I hope, as you become comfortable using this simple but powerful process, you will be on your way to flourishing, living a more fulfilling life, and becoming the next better, happier version of you.

INTRODUCTION

LIFE BY THE INCH

Here's a story about a seventh grader who lived in Southern California.

He was an average kid in every way. He got okay grades, goofed off in the hallways with his friends between classes, rode his bike everywhere, and felt awkward at dances. But there was one thing he was pretty good at—scouting. And he enjoyed it.

He had a sweet part-time job, washing and waxing his grandparents' big blue Buick on the weekends. He got to be around cars and the pay was great—the equivalent of about a hundred dollars today. His parents and grandparents lived near Pasadena. The seven-mile bike ride between them was quite a solo adventure for this 11-year-old.

His grandmother, a wise soul, always took an interest in him. One day, she noticed he seemed kind of down and asked what was wrong. He told her he was really into scouting and wanted to get his Eagle Scout before entering high school. But he couldn't see how he could do it. There was a lot to be done—too many more merit badges and projects to go.

Here's what she said to him.

"You know, Mikey, life by the inch is a cinch, by the mile is a trial."

Wow!

Life by the inch is a cinch, by the mile is a trial.

Yes, that kid was me.

I felt I had hit the wall, but my grandmother knew what I was experiencing was "the marathon in the middle"—the place where a lot of giving up occurs.

I went home and thought about what she said.

Where there had been a blurred field of merit badges and projects stretching over the horizon, patterns emerged. The merit badges arranged themselves into small groups requiring similar efforts or whose subjects were related to one another:

Swimming & Lifesaving
Nature & Birding
Fishing & Kayaking, etc.

INTRODUCTION

A way forward appeared. I scrambled toward it and got busy working on them in small batches. In the summer, before high school, I received my Eagle Scout.

I didn't achieve this because I was wonderful in any way. I wasn't. I did it by using a few of my natural abilities to help me get the badges I needed.

■

Scouting is a lot like life. There are many ways to think and act. To thrive, we need be good in a few essential ones. Scouts have 138 merit badges from which to choose. There are 21, about half of which are required and half elective, required for Eagle.

■

I realized I needed to refine my approach.

The concepts of strengths and competencies were unknown to me. But I probably recognized a couple competencies which would be helpful and supported them with two of my emerging natural strengths. I did not realize it at the time, but these useful

Competency-Strength Combinations

supplied the direction and power I needed to do something meaningful to me.

I needed to become more competent at Developing Plans and Executing Efficiently. Looking back, I likely supported Developing Plans with my Arranger strength, and I supported Executing Efficiently with my Perseverance personal strength. With...

my two Competency-Strength Combinations:

Developing Plans-Arranger
Executing Efficiently-Perseverance,

I was able to use my emerging natural strengths to apply myself to do something meaningful to me.

You've probably heard of strengths, but you may not be too familiar with competencies. Whereas our strengths are of a general nature and can be used in many ways, our competencies focus and amplify our strengths in the direction of specific goals.

In this book, I'll show you how to create and use powerful competency-strength combinations to get your "merit badges" as you become more satisfied and happier with who you are.

■

Do what you can, with what you have, where you are.

– THEODORE ROOSEVELT

INTRODUCTION

Are you ready to take yourself to the next level but feel a bit stuck or overwhelmed? You came to the right place. We are going to help you regain your forward momentum by using a simple but powerful method to become a more fulfilled version of you. Rather than be asked to conform to a one-size-fits-all program, you will learn how to leverage your unique strengths to create potent competencies that will help you make real progress on the important issues in your life.

Confused with all the advice in self-development books?

Me too. Many seem to go too deep with unusable insights into our inner workings, or they tell us to "be like me."

Here you will find a different approach, one that will encourage you to "be more like you."

Think of this as a practical guide to use what you've got to get where you want to go.

You will learn to use:

- *Your strengths* to support the
- *competencies* that will help you
- thrive and
- be a happier, better version of yourself

Using the Level Up Method, you can thrive in *your* way. Pick something which could give you a sense of fulfillment, choose the competency you want to use to get it done, and select the strength of your choice to make it happen.

When we intentionally use our strengths to support our competencies, we can do things more efficiently. An added benefit: It's better for us to be defined by our competencies—the capabilities we use to move forward, than to be announced by our strengths—general areas in which we have potential.

If thriving—being happier and more satisfied with yourself—is desirable, this can help you be more of the person you are capable of being. Here we will show you step-by-step how to make progress on your own personal development, how to form easy-to- understand and highly effective plans, and how to thrive by doing more of what you do best.

With your new approach, you can expect to produce improved results immediately. Here are two scenarios you can consign to the dustbin of history.

INTRODUCTION

HAVE YOU EVER

ONE

Have you ever been disappointed with the results of your efforts or been told you need to improve in some way, then focused on it with remedial training and learning only to find you could not produce the outcome you hoped for?

What happened?

Your approach was probably based on the model of conventional development we have all experienced since an early age—fixing what's wrong with us. We've heard teachers tell pupils to stop doing something. But how many times have we heard a teacher encourage a student to do *more* of something? Problem is, training to minimize weaknesses isn't development, it's damage control. The common approach to weakness fixing, repetitive training without underlying talent, produces mostly disappointment.

Here you will be given permission and encouragement to discover and use more of your natural strengths in a unique way that will improve your capabilities. With the *Level Up* approach, not only will your journey be more pleasant, but it will also be a great deal more effective.

TWO

Have you ever done something in a way that has worked well for you in the past, only to see no meaningful results other than your own depleted energy?

What happened?

You may have been using your natural strengths, a good thing, to address an issue with all the effort you could muster, but were not accurately aiming them at your target. Strengths are very powerful but are general in their nature. To achieve something meaningful, we must be not only powerful, but *specific* in our efforts. When we use *competencies* to *focus our strengths*, we can apply the right amount of energy in precisely the right direction to achieve the results we desire. With The Level Up Method, you will create and apply potent competency-strength combinations to think or do just about anything important to you.

In *Level Up*, you will come to better understand your strengths and how to engage them effectively—by using them to support specific competencies. As you do so, you will optimize the time you spend on tasks, you will expedite your personal development and growth, and you will progress toward reaching your potential.

You will learn how to use your strengths to drive your life in the direction you want it to go.

INTRODUCTION

- Using your strengths to improve your competencies will create *momentum.*
- Momentum gives you *confidence.*
- Behaving and working in a confident manner promotes *optimism.*
- Optimism in action is *enthusiasm.*
- Enthusiasm about who you are leads to *happiness.*

HAPPINESS IS THE GOAL

Did you notice how this progression carries us along to our highest goal, happiness?

> *Happiness is the meaning and purpose of life, The whole aim and end of human existences*
>
> – ARISTOTLE, C. 350 BC

Here, Aristotle is telling us the degree to which we are happy is a fine way to measure how we are living up to our potential as human beings.

Happiness—living well and doing well—is the end goal. When we are thinking and doing competently and flourishing, we are happy.

You are about to embark on a fine journey, during which you will experience small successes early as you change the trajectory of your life.

You will improve your performance, achieving better results sooner and with less wasted effort.

Whenever you use a strength to improve a competency, your enthusiasm will build, and you will propel yourself one step closer to being a happier better, version of you.

Are you ready to Level Up?

CHAPTER 1

THE LEVEL UP METHOD
A New Way to Thrive

> *Life isn't about finding yourself.*
> *Life is about creating yourself.*
>
> – GEORGE BERNARD SHAW

Do you feel you have what it takes to be happier but aren't sure how to unlock your potential? This is perfectly natural. Even high achievers sometimes see their progress flatten out. Often, they just took a wrong turn somewhere. Rather than continuing to climb the path up the mountain, they reached a plateau. Who wants to spend a lot of time and energy only to level off? Here, you will discover how to use the Level Up Method to get you back on the path to thriving in your life.

As our strengths describe *how* we can think, feel, and act, our competencies describe *what* we can do with them.

With the Level Up Method, you will see competencies bring your strengths to life in ways that will help you achieve the results you desire.

Here, you will learn what competencies can do for you and how to select the ones most likely to achieve the results you desire. And you will come to understand how to use your natural strengths to support them to meet almost any challenge.

*As your competencies provide direction,
your strengths supply propulsion.*

You've heard of weapons of destruction? Think of competency-strength combos as your weapons of *con*struction. Use them to make progress on any issue in your life.

Have you ever experienced stress from feeling your life is in charge of you instead of the other way around? Me too.

An additional benefit of incorporating the Level Up Method into your everyday thinking will be the reduction of stress and the increase in self-confidence you experience as you take charge of your life, one competency-strength combo at a time.

In the pages ahead, I will give you many examples of how to use your natural strengths to make progress on the important issues in your life.

CHAPTER 1 - THE LEVEL UP METHOD

CLOSE THE GAP

As you assemble and use your competency-strength combos, you will experience the satisfaction of moving toward the realization of your potential.

A gap analysis is a visual comparison of your actual performance with your potential or desired performance.

    Top line   Where you want to go: your vision, your potential to lead a happy, fulfilling life

    Bottom line Where you will go if you don't change anything

Between the lines is the space to reduce—the difference between the present you and the desired future you. Use the Gap to visualize the actual and possible trajectories of your life.

Just seeing the void between the lines can provide some motivation to take yourself from who you are to who you can become.

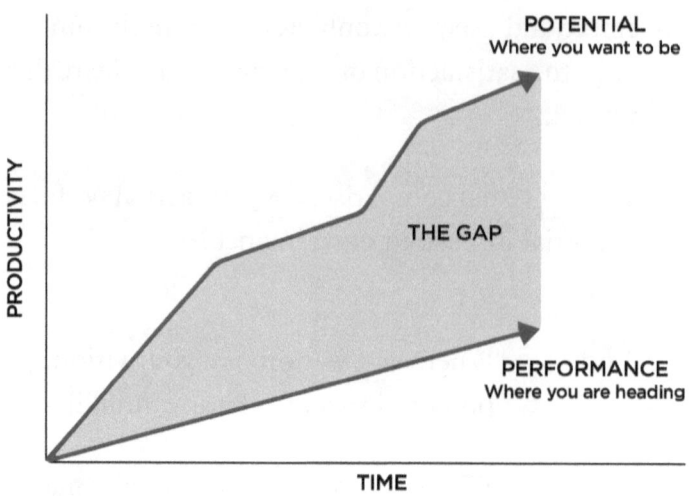

Each of us has a Gap between the vision for ourselves and the reality of where we are. Between the two lie the opportunities for our personal growth.

The Level Up Method and your powerful competency-strength combos will help you make incremental and intentional improvements close the Gap.

What if your progress doesn't resemble the top line in the graph? No one's does. A more accurate portrayal of our lives is this little funny from Demetri Martin:

CHAPTER 1 - THE LEVEL UP METHOD

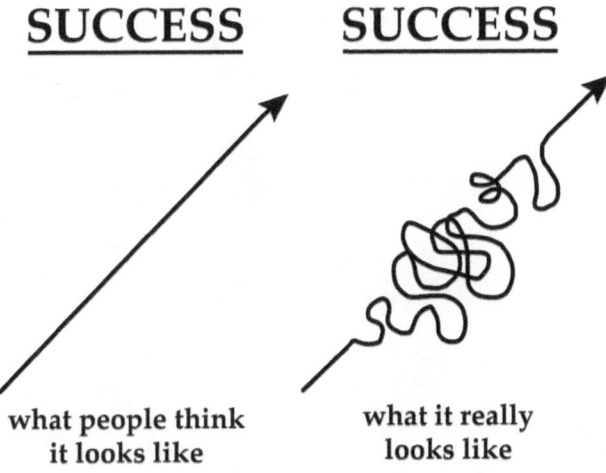

Just keep your focus on your vision and be fine with your squiggle. If you stick with it, it will all work out.

Over time, as you use your natural strengths to become more competent, you will find yourself more often at the top of your game. Your ability to repeatedly produce positive results will improve and your Gap will shrink.

Now, let's crack open the strengths library and discover how to use the unique and mighty abilities each of us has.

PART I

YOUR STRENGTHS
You Are Unique

> *Hide not your talents. They for use were made. What is a sundial in the shade?*
>
> – BENJAMIN FRANKLIN

The desirable aspects of your character, and the unique ways you solve problems and work with others, are your strengths. Your most potent ones are called your signature strengths.

This section provides a general understanding of strengths, and sets the stage for how you will use them to improve your competencies with the Level Up Method.

Imagine you have your own personal store—a nice one.

Stocked on the shelves of your store are your strengths. The premium items, your most potent strengths, are on the upper shelves, between your head and chest. Most of your strengths are on the shelves in the middle. Many useful items are here. The few on the lower shelves mostly just sit there, gathering dust.

Other people also have stores, but nobody has a store exactly like yours.

You may use the items in your store however you wish—for yourself, to share with others, or to offer for sale. But, unlike the items in a real store, whenever you take your strengths off the shelf and use them, they not only remain on the shelf, but get better, like some *Alice in Wonderland* paradox.

In this chapter, you will see how to discover and utilize the *personal* strengths that define your character—your mental and moral qualities—and the *performance* strengths you can draw upon to accomplish things, alone or with others.

PART I - YOUR STRENGTHS

FIRST, IDENTIFY YOUR STRENGTHS

Strengths are tasks or actions you can do well. These include knowledge, proficiencies, skills, and talents. People use their traits and abilities to complete work, relate with others, and achieve goals.[1]

How do you know what your own strengths are, and whether they're chest high, knee high, or at ankle level on your figurative store shelves?

With some reflection and intuition, you may be able to create a list of your strengths.

Or you can take an assessment. We'll talk about the two best assessments shortly.

To identify your highest personal strengths, think of times when you felt most alive. What were you doing? Were you alone, with others, at work, at play?

What words described how you felt or acted at these times?

These are your strengths.

1: YourDictionary, s.v. "Examples of Strengths", July 6 2022
https://examples.yourdictionary.com/examples-of-strengths.html

In *Level Up*, we explore the two major types of strengths each of us has:

Personal strengths
These describe how you think, feel, and behave

Performance strengths
These define work you are capable of doing alone or with others

CONSIDER TAKING A STRENGTHS ASSESSMENT...

Take a *quantitative* approach. With an online assessment or two, see what a trusted survey says about you.

To learn what our *personal* strengths are, I like the free VIA Character Strengths Survey. Plan to spend about 25 minutes taking this. It will provide insights into which of the 24 personal strengths most define you as a person. You can find it at www.viacharacter.org.

To learn what our performance strengths are, my favorite assessment is CliftonStrengths®[2] from Gallup. It will take you about 40 minutes and will reflect your talents in 34 categories of performance strengths. You can find it at www.gallup.com.

---

[2]: formerly called StrengthsFinder

A feature I appreciate about both is VIA and Gallup name the strengths with common terms that accurately capture their essence.

Almost 100 million people have taken the VIA and Gallup strengths surveys. Ninety percent of Fortune 500 companies use them.

■

I think of Gallup's 34 performance strengths and VIA's 24 personal strengths as the two halves of our strengths sphere. Collectively, they form a cohesive whole, with no gaps and very little overlay.

THE STRENGTHS SPHERE

It's nice how they fit together.

...OR DIY

Take a qualitative approach and create your own list of the strengths which best describe your natural qualities.

Entering "strengths" in your search bar will produce links with hundreds of names for strengths identified by different sources.

For a list of the 58 strengths we explore in *Level Up*, see the Index at the back of the book.

Whether you create your own list of strengths or learn them from an assessment, enjoy the process of discovering which ones most accurately describe your abilities.

If you are artistically inclined, consider your strengths as you would the keys on a piano.

If 24 personal strengths and 34 performance strengths sound like a lot to deal with, think of how you can draw upon these 58 strengths as pianists use the 88 keys on a piano; they do not attempt to use every possible note, but play select combinations that produce all kinds of wonderful results.

The pianist doesn't play all 88 keys. She plays in the range where she can use her abilities and feelings in a way that most pleases the audience and herself. Think of yourself as a musician who can produce beautiful and original music within a range. Learning your talents will help you identify the notes that are the best ones for you to use when making *your* music. You get

PART I - YOUR STRENGTHS

to decide what kind of music you wish to make. Adventurous? Contemplative? Romantic? It can be any of these or something else. Your choice. When you play the pieces you want to play, your practice will be more productive and enjoyable because you are using your strengths in the best way—with intention.

Playing your music your way, you engage the strengths which are the most useful, natural, and pleasurable to use. Irving Berlin never learned to play the piano and only played in F-sharp. With only 36 black keys to choose from, look what he did with what *he* had![3]

Whether you use the 58 personal and professional strengths from VIA and Gallup or the ones on a list of your own making, here's a simple process to detect which ones will be most useful to you.

3: Irving Berlin (1888–1989) was an Israeli-born American composer and lyricist. During his 60-year career, he wrote an estimated 1,500 songs, including scores for Broadway shows and Hollywood films. Berlin is widely considered one of the greatest songwriters in American history, despite his extremely limited piano skills.

NEXT, SORT YOUR STRENGTHS

An interesting and revealing exercise is to divide your personal strengths and your professional strengths into three tiers.

TOP TIER

Your Signature Strengths—these are "always on" for you

Starting with the top strengths in one of your reports, or from your own list built from your experiences and intuition, draw a line under the group of strengths you use most frequently and effectively. These are the ones most likely to reside in your top quartile. You may find you have around six signature personal strengths and approximately eight signature performance strengths.

BOTTOM TIER

Your Lesser Strengths—unlikely to be of much use to you

Starting at the bottom, draw a line *over* the group of strengths you rarely use. These are your lesser strengths. These probably dwell in your bottom quartile. You may find six lesser personal strengths and eight lesser performance strengths down on this shelf. They are infrequently of much use to you, and we are not going to make any attempt to elevate them. Just acknowledge their position and move on. Some strengths must be at the bottom. These are yours.

PART I - YOUR STRENGTHS

MIDDLE TIER

Your Intermediate Strengths—the big group in the middle

Use these to add some extra power to your signature strengths.

USE YOUR STRENGTHS WHERE THEY CAN BE OF THE MOST BENEFIT TO YOU

The Level Up Method will help you intentionally engage your strengths to improve your competencies and thrive in your life. But how to know which strengths to use for what?

We have for you here a structure, the Five Sets of Strengths, to organize your strengths in the groups where they help you think or act. In each of the next chapters, we will explore one of the Five Sets of Strengths.

The Five Sets of Strengths

THINKING
CONNECTING
ENABLING
PERFORMING
BELIEVING

We will see how your personal strengths and your performance strengths can be useful to you in each set as you solve problems, interact with others, get stuff done, and become the next better version of you.

Rather than a rigid prescriptive system, consider this a flexible set of suggested homes for your strengths.

For reference, in the Appendix, you will find the Five Sets of Strengths and the personal and performance strengths within each set.

THE W WORD
WHAT ABOUT WEAKNESSES?

> *Success is achieved by developing our strengths, not by eliminating our weaknesses.*
>
> – MARILYN VOS SAVANT,
> HOLDER OF HIGHEST RECORDED IQ

A weakness is anything that impedes your success. If you engage in it, it will drain your energy and block you from being productive. Weaknesses can't be fixed. They can only be managed. Get a little better at them, work around them, or leave them be.

Your lesser strengths may be among them. If you can, just avoid using them.

Remember, it's only a weakness if it gets in your way. If it doesn't cause you to step on a rake, let it go. Here's Coach

John Wooden on the subject: "Do not let what you cannot do interfere with what you can do."

Most of us enjoy doing things we're good at. The things we don't enjoy doing? We're probably not very good at them. From a strengths perspective, we should be spending our time and energies elsewhere. Yet we are often directed to fix what's wrong with us. "Opportunities for improvement," they're called.

Those things you don't do well? You now have permission to stop doing them!

Have you ever heard a parent tell a child he can be anything he wants to be?

Here's the catch—actually, we *can't* be anything we want to be.

The idea that everyone can be anything they want to be if they work hard to fix their weaknesses leads to a lot of frustration and wasted effort that could have been better used in the service of strengths.

Improvement requires persistence, but the danger of repetitive training that does not engage a natural strength is burnout.

Focusing on weaknesses leads to frustration.
Focusing on strengths leads to success.

For many of us, the tendency during our entire lives has been to focus on our weaknesses—at school, at work, and in our relationships. For a perspective on how this came to be, see the "Fixing Weaknesses Goes Way Back" piece at the end of the chapter.

In school, test scores reflected what we did *not* know. Except for essay tests, they provided few insights into the areas where we excelled. Contrast this conventional development approach with strengths-based development.

Conventional Development	*Strengths-Based Development*
Identify areas of weakness	Identify areas of strength
Reduce your weaknesses	Develop and use your strengths

But there is one weakness of which we should be wary.

> **Our greatest weakness lies in giving up. The most certain way to succeed is always to try just one more time.**
>
> – THOMAS EDISON

Thomas Edison and Henry Ford were friends. In 1929, Henry Ford built Greenfield Village in Dearborn, a suburb of Detroit. For this museum of American innovation, Ford acquired many of Edison's artifacts and one of his power plants. He used them to recreate Edison's Menlo Park Complex. It was in this New Jersey laboratory that Edison perfected the lightbulb in 1880. If you haven't been to Greenfield, consider it for your bucket list. For his demonstration town, Ford assembled a village of buildings and inventions from the Who's Who of the late 19th and early 20th century industries.

Fun fact: Edison and Ford were members of a traveling mastermind group, The Vagabonds. Other members were President Warren G. Harding, Harvey Firestone, and Luther Burbank. Imagine if you were invited to attend one of their meetings.

Strolling through Edison's laboratory produces hushed wonderment among the visitors. Even children, sensing that something important happened here, become calm. It's a very simple and humble place. But what strikes you is that this is a place where real work, the unglamorous kind, was done.

His work reminds us to try, try, then try again. With ordinary materials and incredible persistence, Edison tried to produce the uncommon. Eventually, he perfected the lightbulb, and the world changed.

Outside the building is this sign:

> **I never did anything by accident, nor did any of my inventions come by accident. They came by work.**
>
> – THOMAS EDISON, INVENTOR

What strengths do you think Edison possessed? His personal strengths of Curiosity, Creativity, and Perseverance must have been off the charts. Likewise, for his performance strengths, Analytical and Achiever.

Only Edison could be Edison, of course. But we all can do the work—to burn brighter and longer while using less energy.

In Part II: The Competencies, we will reveal 17 productive ways you can apply your strengths to thrive and live a happier life. These competencies will provide the conduits through which your strengths will flow as you make progress on the things that are important to you. Doing so, you will begin to harness your potential.

PART I - YOUR STRENGTHS

FIXING WEAKNESSES GOES WAY BACK

Since their introduction, codes of conduct and laws have been steadying influences on our baser inclinations, our weaknesses, if you will. When people interact, they need guidelines to maintain order.

Fifty centuries ago, the richest and most densely populated place in the world was Mesopotamia, the area between the Tigris and Euphrates. Around the 32nd century BC, the Sumerians invented writing. A thousand years later, in the 22nd century BC, they created the first laws. Just to the north, around the 18th century BC, King Hammurabi developed Babylonian law. If you broke these laws, no "three hots and a cot" in some cushy prison for you. You paid the price immediately. An eye for an eye.

About 1,500 miles to the southwest of Mesopotamia is Mt. Sinai, where Moses received the 10 Commandments. They are thought to have been written somewhere between the 16th and 13th centuries BC. The 10 Commandments were not exactly laws, but neither were they the 10 Suggestions. At least they, unlike laws, encouraged you to do *more* of some things, two to be exact.

Fast forward to modern times and us in our formative years.

From our parents, our schools, and the organizations in our young lives, a what-not-to-do approach to life is baked into us at an early age.

When you finally get your driver's license and have your first real taste of freedom, you get a whole new set of thou-shalt-nots to deal with.

It probably has to be this way until we become responsible adults. Our early years are spent in human growth—maturing physically, cognitively, and socially. At adulthood, we can transition from human growth to personal development, the subject of our book.

But the Mesopotamians didn't have the chance for much personal development. With average lifespans of 30 years, they spent most of their years growing up and needing rules to keep them from leading with their weaknesses.

With our longer lifetimes, we are more fortunate. Once we tip from human development to personal development, we can concentrate less on tamping down our weaknesses and more on turning up our strengths. This is where the real pleasure of adulthood begins.

CHAPTER 2

THINKING

Increase Your Wisdom

with your Personal Strengths[4]

CREATIVITY   CURIOSITY   JUDGEMENT

LOVE OF LEARNING   PERSPECTIVE

with your Performance Strengths[5]

ANALYTICAL   CONTEXT   FUTURISTIC

IDEATION   INPUT   INTELLECTION

LEARNER   STRATEGIC

4: from the VIA Institute
5: from Gallup, Inc.

We begin our exploration of strengths with those residing in our Thinking set. We'll address each of these 13 strengths with a look at:

- the signals it sends
- what it feels like
- how to use it

Each of our strengths within the Thinking set can be useful when creating our vision, processing information, making decisions, and forming the plans to do the things we want to do.

TAKE IT EASY…

Please don't feel you have to study every entry in this and the other chapters on our strengths. If you are reading this for yourself, you may wish to focus on just your top "signature" strengths. If you are helping others use their strengths, these passages can serve as ready references as you guide them.

THINKING WITH YOUR PERSONAL STRENGTHS

CREATIVITY

The ones who ask, "I wonder what would happen if...?" are likely blessed with the strength of Creativity. They are always looking for new ways to do things.

If this sounds like you, you love bringing new concepts and strategies into your life and to the lives of others you care about.. Your Creativity broadens your outlook on the ways to become the best version of you.

Use your Creativity to bring new perspectives to artistic expression and to help others see new ways to consider issues they are facing.

CURIOSITY

When Columbus set sail, he was under no delusion the earth was flat. That idea was resolved by Pythagoras in 500 BC. But Columbus, and his sponsor Queen Isabella, did have a great deal of curiosity about the potential for a lucrative western trade route to China. If he knew that the sparsely populated North American continent was to be in his way, we would probably not be celebrating Columbus Day.

With Curiosity, you have a natural interest in pursuing new information and experiences to deepen your understanding of a variety of subjects.

Use your Curiosity to explore, investigate, and learn new things about any topic of interest to you. Think of your Curiosity strength as your "license to learn."

JUDGEMENT

If Judgement is one of your signature strengths, you carefully examine all the facts and issues that will help you make an objective decision. You consider each bit of relevant information from multiple points of view before concluding an analysis.

Your ability to think critically, to weigh all the evidence, is rooted firmly in our Thinking set of strengths. With few preconceived ideas about how to best address a new issue, you carefully consider all the facts before making your choice of the best way to proceed.

LOVE OF LEARNING

Someone who enjoys visiting museums and taking classes where they can learn new things, deeply appreciates the acquisition of new information and experiences.

While others may be bored by the absence of activity associated with acquiring new information, you are excited about the mental and emotional stimulation it brings.

Pulling at the thread of a fresh concept on the internet can bring a whole new tapestry onto your screen. Next thing you know, it's two hours later.

PERSPECTIVE

Do you know someone who is a "big picture person," one to whom the world makes more sense than to the rest of us? He is likely one who has Perspective, the gift of a broad point of view.

If this sounds like you, when you listen to a presentation or a conversation your mind takes into consideration many other things that help frame the subject—your experiences with it, how it compares with similar concepts, and how it could help you live a more fulfilling life.

Use your Perspective to see the big picture. We choose to see mostly what's directly in front of us. But, if we extend our arms away from our body, we may be able to see our fingertips when they are 180° apart. That's peripheral vision, and it shows us how broad our field of vision can be. When you are charging full speed ahead, look out the window to your left and right occasionally to gain a sense of what's around you.

THINKING WITH YOUR PERFORMANCE STRENGTHS

ANALYTICAL

Analytical people tend to take a practical point of view rather than an emotional one. Think of those who ask all the questions. As they do, and their questions are answered, the rest of us learn a little more about the topic. Always on the side of truth, Analytical people are objective problem solvers and make decisions based upon the evidence.

If this sounds like you, you bring logic into your life. Your ability to apply rigorous attention to an issue often reveals patterns and connections between its different aspects. You use your natural investigative ability to sort through information, organize it, and make it more understandable for others.

CONTEXT

Gallup tells us those with the strength Context can compare the past to the present. They can see the chain of events leading to where we are today.

If you can think contextually, you value experience and the lessons learned from the past. You can see the connections between past-present-future progressions and can use what happened in the past to open up opportunities in the present and make plans for your future.

When you think with Context, you can pull from the experiences of others and yourself to solve problems as they arise. In so doing, you help ensure that mistakes made yesterday will not be repeated tomorrow.

FUTURISTIC

Those who are drawn to thinking about what the future might hold are energized more by what can be more than by what is.

If you naturally enjoy thinking about what is to come, you are inspired by what the future may bring. You anticipate what could happen and can imagine it in vivid detail. You can see it so clearly that, sometimes, the present feels like the past.

Most strengths can be used to push you in a direction you want to go. With your forward thinking, you feel pulled toward your vision of what is possible.

IDEATION

Those who ask, "What if...?" consider issues from multiple perspectives and can generate new ideas around any topic. As they form ideas and concepts, they often put a new spin on things, broadening the ways in which a subject is considered and evaluated.

If this sounds like you, you can generate new ideas of your own on a variety of subjects. When you do, you enjoy considering the new perspectives you bring to existing concepts. You have the ability to connect existing ideas and consider concepts not previously considered.

Use your Ideation to bring new thinking and new views to the table for further consideration. Your constant pursuit of creation enables you to see things from multiple points of view.

INPUT

The ones who say, "Tell me more..." love gathering new information, sorting, and storing it.

If this sounds like you, you enjoy collecting facts, objects, and experiences. You always want to know more. By nature, you are inquisitive. You enjoy performing research and absorbing information that may be useful later. You love to acquire knowledge about a wide variety of topics.

Seek new experiences where you can use your inquisitive nature to deepen your understanding of a subject, expanding what you already know about it.

INTELLECTION

Those who say, "Let me think about it and get back to you" naturally enjoy the process of more deeply understanding things. They are conscientious and often bring perspective and insights that others may have missed.

If Intellection is one of your strengths, you like to think. When lost in your thoughts, you feel bliss. Quiet reflection is a favorite activity, considering what transpired in the past and what is to come.

When and where you use this strength of understanding is important, because there are likely times, places, or activities where you make your best discoveries. When you replicate these situations, you promote thinking in pleasurable and useful ways. You enjoy pondering topics you know something about, then furthering your understanding of those subjects. You take your time to consider a project before initiating action.

LEARNER

The ones who say, "Let me look into that" love the process of discovery. They will put in the time and effort to investigate a new concept.

If this sounds like you, you are naturally inquisitive. Self-improvement is important and you enjoy exploring new topics. You are confident taking on new challenges and helping others discover more about a subject. You are delighted to be on journeys that take you from not knowing to knowing.

STRATEGIC

When making plans, those who ask, "How does this work...?" want to see the big picture. They are creative, conceptual, can spot the underlying themes of an issue, and organize them to achieve desirable outcomes.

If this sounds like you, you can naturally spot patterns, identify the alternatives, and form the plans that make the most sense.

Trust your insights and put your ideas to work. When you use your broad perspective to consider challenges and opportunities, approach them as you would when playing a board game. Thinking several steps ahead, you can make the moves that will best set you up for a fulfilling win. Seeing the desired result helps you find the best path to get from where you are to where you want to go.

CHAPTER 3

CONNECTING

Engage with People and Support Them

with your Personal Strengths[6]

FAIRNESS HONESTY LOVE

SOCIAL INTELLIGENCE TEAMWORK

with your Performance Strengths[7]

EMPATHY HARMONY INCLUDER

INDIVIDUALIZATION POSITIVITY RELATOR

6: from the VIA Institute
7: from Gallup, Inc.

When we understand others' needs and feelings, we can connect more deeply with them. Strong relationships bind people together.

We'll address each of the 11 Connecting strengths with a look at:

- the signals it sends
- what it feels like
- how to use it

Each of these strengths can be valuable when you are engaging with others.

CONNECTING WITH YOUR PERSONAL STRENGTHS

FAIRNESS

Fairness is the quality we want our deities and judges to have. They use it to treat everyone the same and uniformly interpret how the laws apply to the parties in a dispute.

When you treat people fairly, you bring an absence of personal bias and an abundance of impartiality to your interactions. You are equitable and considerate of one and all.

With all of life's distractions, this strength can take conscious effort to maintain. A fine example of how we can help ourselves be fairer is a device used in the audition process for musicians who wish to join an orchestra. As the small selection committee sits near the center of the hall, each aspiring musician performs behind a screen. Short, tall, male, female, plump, trim... none of that matters. All that counts is how they play.

Fairness helps us remove irrelevant details and opinions and enables us to consider only essential information when making decisions that affect others.

HONESTY

If you know someone who can be counted upon to speak the truth, you are probably acquainted with one whose beliefs and behaviors demonstrate he feels that "honesty is the best policy."[8]

If this sounds like you, you are sincere and straightforward with yourself and others.

If Honesty is one of your signature strengths, you make a trustworthy companion on any journey.

Use your Honesty to consistently demonstrate your integrity and dependability to others. In return, they will give you their confidence.

---

[8]: Sir Edwin Sandys, in the English settlement of Jamestown, Virginia, said it first in 1599. Two hundred years later, Benjamin Franklin used it in a comparison of Great Britain to America.

LOVE

Do you know someone who highly values their strongest relationships? Chances are you are acquainted with a person whose signature strengths include Love. Not ones to play it close to the vest, those who feel and exhibit Love openly share with others their true feelings.

If this sounds like you, you have the need and ability to connect with others in ways where all can demonstrate their care for one another. You radiate warmth and appreciate it when others do the same.

Use your strength of Love to bring you closer to those who matter most. Using the strength of Love is a powerful way to create and maintain strong give-and-take relationships.

SOCIAL INTELLIGENCE

If you are acquainted with one who can read a room and always knows the right thing to say, you have seen Social Intelligence in action. Those with this strength understand the thoughts and feelings of others around them and are tactful when speaking with them.

If this sounds like you, you appreciate what is different about others. This enables you to deal with a variety of people and maintain sturdy relationships with them.

CHAPTER 3 - CONNECTING

TEAMWORK

If you are fortunate enough to know someone who "plays well with others," you know a team player—one who enjoys working with people to achieve a common goal. Teamwork is the strength that helps us collaborate with others to reach a shared objective.

If this sounds like you, you are loyal to your team and committed to doing what you can to help it be successful. When you are with your team, you put the priorities of the team above your own. Then you get busy and do your part to help the team reach its goal. Being a valued member of a productive team is an often-cited contributor to personal fulfillment and happiness.

With your Teamwork strength, you feel more alive and engaged in your group activities. Teamwork isn't just for sports or business. It is for any activity where you join with another. You and your study buddy are a team. You and your passenger on a road trip are a team. And you and your significant other are a team, one that probably has plans for a lot of happiness in the future.

CONNECTING WITH YOUR PERFORMANCE STRENGTHS

EMPATHY

The person who says, "I feel your pain" is one who senses the emotions of others and can speak up for those whose voices are not being heard.

If this sounds like you, you are intuitive and can understand the feelings of others. With Empathy, you can form relationships of great emotional depth.

When you use this emotional intelligence to communicate with others, you do so with an understanding of their feelings and points of view. This provides them the comfort that you are with them on their journey.

HARMONY

Those who, in a heated discussion, say, "Okay, let's take it down a notch" believe in the value of togetherness. They help us see that what we have in common is more powerful than our differences.

If this sounds like you, you are more interested in what unites us than what divides us. You find conflict to be unproductive and look for areas of agreement with others in your life.

CHAPTER 3 - CONNECTING

Use your Harmony to connect with others and help them reach a common understanding. When people, organizations and countries find themselves in agreement about the positive nature of their relationship, joy is soon to follow.

INCLUDER

Those who have *All Are Welcome Here* doormats want everyone to be on the inside.

If you have an inclusive attitude, you accept a wide variety of people. You feel we are at our best when everyone is involved and working together. You believe all are equally important and you want to widen the circle.

Engage your Includer to bring tolerance and acceptance to any gathering. You hospitable nature makes you a natural at bringing people into a group. As you accept and welcome others, you help them feel valued for who they are.

INDIVIDUALIZATION

The one who says, "You know what you would be good at?" can sense what is unique and different about people, what their preferences are, and what they do well. He sees every person as one of a kind.

If this sounds like you, you know different people have different needs and you personalize your relationships with each. You want to give others what they need and appreciate the most.

As you recognize what is special about others, you draw out the best in them. You can find out what they do well and help them do it.

POSITIVITY

Ever notice how some people seem to light up a room when they enter? Their optimistic nature has a stimulating and confidence-building effect on others. Their sociability, warmth, and energy make others feel safe and supported.

If this sounds like you, you are quick to smile, generous with praise, and love to laugh. Your contagious enthusiasm brings energy to any relationship or gathering. People want to be near you because their world looks better when you are around.

As you demonstrate your positive attitude, you inspire others to also look at the bright side. Sensing your optimism, they feel happier and more hopeful.

CHAPTER 3 - CONNECTING

RELATOR

The friend who lifts her head and smiles when you arrive is likely one who enjoys nurturing her closest relationships. She is more interested in heartfelt and durable connections than in making casual acquaintances.

If this sounds like you, you value solid, genuine, and mutually rewarding relationships with others. You are drawn to people you already know and like to spend time with them. You enjoy quiet moments with people you deeply trust. As others see that you value true friendships and keep confidences, they perceive you as more trustworthy.

To sustain connection with those important to you, spend time together to share your feelings and experiences. As a prolonged and thorough study by Harvard University concluded, "Good relationships keep us happier and healthier. Period."[9]

9: "The Importance of Deep Relationships", Tal Ben-Shahar Ph.D., Psychology Today, May 12, 2020

CHAPTER 4

ENABLING

Have a Positive Effect on People

with your Personal Strengths[10]

FORGIVENESS   HUMILITY   HUMOR

KINDNESS   LEADERSHIP

with your Performance Strengths[11]

COMMUNICATION   DEVELOPER   SELF-ASSURANCE

SIGNIFICANCE   WOO

10: from the VIA Institute
11: from Gallup, Inc.

When you demonstrate you care about others and are willing to help, it has a positive effect on them.

We'll address each of the 10 Enabling strengths with a look at:

- the signals it sends
- what it feels like
- how to use it

The Enabling strengths help you show others the concern you have for them and can prepare them to see the benefits of your perspectives.

ENABLING WITH YOUR PERSONAL STRENGTHS

FORGIVENESS

Those who refer to past injustices and slights as "water under the bridge" are demonstrating their signature strength of Forgiveness. Using this strength promotes equanimity with others.

Forgiveness, which involves letting go of resentment, is closely related to mercy, which includes showing compassion instead of punishing people for their behavior.

When you forgive others, you show you can move forward from less-than-benevolent treatment. Overcome resentment and maintain a positive attitude by not letting minor offenses affect you.

Remember, Forgiveness is a strength that doesn't require forgetting. Forgive and forget is not always the best advice. Perhaps to forgive and learn is better advice.

HUMILITY

Those who allow their accomplishments to speak for themselves are signaling their strength of Humility. Not only do they not *act* as if they are more special than others, they don't *feel* more special than others.

If this sounds like you, then when you find yourself in the spotlight, you move. Letting others have their turn is more important than bringing attention to yourself. It's not about being shy or lacking confidence. It's quite the opposite. The strength of Humility is a clear indicator of a healthy self-esteem.

Use your Humility to send the message you are a modest person. Most people aren't fond of braggarts, but they admire those who avoid drawing attention to themselves.

HUMOR

Do you know someone who can bring a smile to your face and brighten your day? The most likely reason is that they possess Humor as a signature strength. Humor prefers a lighter approach, chipping away at unwarranted seriousness.

Use your Humor to add balance to any conversation or gathering. The strength of Humor is less about being the life of the party and more about the sense of lightness and levity you can bring.

KINDNESS

Do you know someone who consistently "plays nice"? When she does so, her compassion and care for others has a positive effect on them, demonstrating that Kindness is among her signature strengths.

If this sounds like you, you enjoy doing things for others. Those hundreds of little things you do, they make a difference. Can you imagine a world with too much kindness? Me neither.

Use your Kindness to show your awareness of others' needs. Let it remain your secret that you are the one who benefits most when you help them.

CHAPTER 4 - ENABLING

LEADERSHIP

If you don't know any natural-born leaders, maybe it's because there aren't any. Warren Bennis, who served on the faculties of Harvard and Boston University, discovered that leaders are made, not born.[12] And most leaders are self-made. This is good news for those of us who want to increase our strength of Leadership.

If you are one who uses your Leadership strength, you enjoy the challenge of bringing others together to get things done. Creating a vision, setting achievable goals, assembling work groups, keeping others' sense of fulfillment up, and accomplishing what you set out to do are rewarding activities.

Use your Leadership strength to organize and guide any effort that will benefit from having multiple participants work on a common goal. Whether it be in your community, or in your profession, the world needs more leaders. There are positions open everywhere at every level. If you see an unfulfilled need for leadership somewhere, maybe you are the one who can fill it.

12: "The most dangerous leadership myth is that leaders are born—that there is a genetic factor to leadership. This myth asserts that people simply either have certain charismatic qualities or not. That's nonsense; in fact, the opposite is true. Leaders are made rather than born. And the way we become leaders is by learning about leadership through life and job experiences, not with university degrees," Warren Bennis, *Managing People Is Like Herding Cats* (Provo, UT: Executive Excellence Publishing, 1999), 163.

ENABLING WITH YOUR PERFORMANCE STRENGTHS

COMMUNICATION

Do you know someone who has a way with words? Chances are he can put his thoughts and feelings into vivid word pictures that bring clarity and understanding to a topic.

If this sounds like you, you have an ability to express your thoughts in writing and speaking. You love to tell stories and make connections with others. You are a good listener and a good conversationalist. You can craft just the right message for any audience and can serve as an effective spokesperson for the ideas and opinions of others.

To use your strength of Communication, practice getting your message across. Find opportunities to think aloud or in writing. Study the effect it has, then refine it. As you do so, you will improve your ability to capture the attention of others and be understood.

DEVELOPER

The ones who are always looking for ways to help people improve love inspiring and motivating them to become better versions of themselves.

CHAPTER 4 - ENABLING

If this sounds like you, you see what others can become. To you, people can realize their potential when they are provided the opportunities and encouragement to thrive. You feel everyone can be on a path to getting better. When you can participate in someone's process of improvement, you feel energized.

As you help others improve themselves, they will begin to gain the most sustainable kind of forward motion—that which is generated internally.

SELF-ASSURANCE

Those who say, "We can do this!" are comfortable going first. They bravely lead the way, inspiring others to trust them. This can have a contagious positive effect on those around them, who will feel a boost to their own confidence.

If this sounds like you, you deeply trust your instincts and are comfortable with your decisions. You are confident in your ability to live your own life. Your internal guidance system enables you to be independent and self-governing. You know you can take on challenges, address issues as they appear, and produce results.

Comfortable with risk, you can use your intuition and certainty to bring a sense of order in times of chaos. Others appreciate the clarity and stability you bring to volatile situations.

SIGNIFICANCE

Think of those who want to make a difference want to be recognized for doing work that is meaningful and of lasting value to others. They desire to be noticed, heard, and appreciated. They avoid unimportant tasks and spend their time doing the things that matter most. Those with the strength Significance feel a need to be admired as credible, professional, and successful.

Use your strength of Significance to make contributions that will have a positive effect on others. Your determination to make the world a better place inspires and motivates them to reach for outcomes they may not have considered.

WOO: "WINNING OTHERS OVER"

Ever notice how some people can start relationships and build rapport quickly and easily? They know how to form positive connections with others by breaking the ice with a hearty welcome or melting it with their personal warmth.

If this sounds like you, you love meeting new people. You are charming, open, and create a space of social comfort for others.

When you transfer your enthusiasm to them, they feel included and more at ease.

CHAPTER 4 - ENABLING

Insert yourself into situations where you can be around people. It will energize you and give you opportunities to broaden your network. Volunteer to be a greeter at events of any kind. Your warmth and openness will make the attendees feel welcome.

CHAPTER 5

PERFORMING
Do Your Best

with your Personal Strengths[13]

BRAVERY   PERSEVERANCE   PRUDENCE

SELF-REGULATION   ZEST

with your Performance Strengths[14]

ACHIEVER   ACTIVATOR   ADAPTABILITY
ARRANGER   COMMAND   COMPETITION
CONSISTENCY   DELIBERATIVE   DISCIPLINE
FOCUS   MAXIMIZER   RESPONSIBILITY
                   RESTORATIVE

13: from the VIA Institute
14: from Gallup, Inc.

When superior results are needed, these strengths will help you put your thoughts and plans into action, Your Performing strengths can help you get things done in ways that are satisfying and rewarding

We'll address each of these 18 Performing strengths with a look at:

- the signals it sends
- what it feels like
- how to use it

Your Performing with Excellence strengths give you the stamina to stay on track and see things through to their successful completion.

PERFORMING WITH YOUR PERSONAL STRENGTHS

BRAVERY

When King Henry V implored, "Once more into the breach, dear friends, once more"[15] he was exhibiting just about all we need to know about the strength of Bravery.

15: William Shakespeare, Henry V, 3.1.1. References are to act, scene, and line. Henry is rallying his troops to attack an enemy city through a gap in the wall that surrounds it.

If this sounds like something you would say, you see threats and opportunities as challenges and face them head on. Fear is something you can push through in service of reaching your desired destination.

Use your Bravery to subordinate anxiety to a level where you can objectively weigh the potential risks and rewards before you make a decision. Bravery is not the absence of fear. Rather, it is the willingness to act despite it. Some of the most decorated military pilots, praised for their heroism, admitted to being frightened every time they got in their plane. Whether it is an external physical fear—fire, for example—or an inner mental or emotional one, setting fear to the side for a while can help you see further down the road toward your destination.

Did you notice we define bravery by squarely facing not only threats, but opportunities? If you perceive something big may be coming your way, use your Bravery to help you evaluate your options. It is human nature to become as paralyzed by big opportunities as it is by big perceived threats. Few of us can fly through the Alps in our wingsuits, but we can and should seize the opportunities that come our way. As Eleanor Roosevelt said, "Do one thing every day that scares you."

PERSEVERANCE

When American journalist Jim Watkins said, "A river cuts through rock not because of its power, but because of its persistence," he reminds us that perseverance, not power, is the key to achieving the results we want in our lives. People with the strength of Perseverance enjoy finishing what they start.

If *you* can cut through rock, you keep moving despite obstacles in your way. You stay the course. The grind of life? It gives you pleasure. You use your Perseverance to stay organized and see things through to completion.

Use your strength of Perseverance as the Energizer Bunny uses his batteries. They help him keep going, and going, and going…

PRUDENCE

John Heywood's quote, "Look before you leap,"[16] reminds us to exercise the strength of Prudence to avoid taking unnecessary risks.

16: The first English language version of this appeared in 1546, in a collection of proverbs produced by John Heywood, a musician and playwright in Tudor, England. In a few pages, you will see another one of the many translated by Heywood. Others include "a bird in the hand is worth two in the bush," "beggars can't be choosers," "let sleeping dogs lie," "the more the merrier," "can't see the forest for the trees," and another famous one that will appear in the next chapter.

CHAPTER 5 - PERFORMING

If you look before you leap, you are careful about the choices you make and exhibit restraint in your life. Think of your Prudence as "wise caution."[17]

Engage your Prudence to govern yourself by the use of reason. Weigh the pluses and minuses of different thoughts, feelings, and actions to steer clear of avoidable mishaps in life. Examine the cost and benefit of each option before jumping headlong into something.

SELF-REGULATION

When Lao Tzu said, "The best fighter is never angry,"[18] he demonstrated the importance of using our Self-Regulation strength. Our ability to make choices is a key source of life's enjoyment.

We've all made both wise and foolish decisions, but those who use their strength of Self-Regulation are able to make measured decisions which promote balance and order in their lives.

When you activate your Self-Regulation, you summon the self-control to detour gratification from thoughts or actions that will not serve you well.

17: Ryan M. Niemiec and Robert E. McGrath, The Power of Character Strengths (Cincinnati, OH: Via Institute on Character, 2019).
18: c. 600 BC

ZEST

Our Zest strength supports our enthusiasm to enjoy life at every opportunity.

If you are zestful, you willingly bring energy and excitement to the things you do. You feel alive and invigorated by the ideas you have, the people you know, and the projects you are committed to.

When you want a bit more spice in your life, just add your Zest to any desirable endeavor. You'll have a more positive attitude and a stronger connection with what truly matters in life.

PERFORMING WITH YOUR PROFESSIONAL STRENGTHS

ACHIEVER

George Mallory's explanation for climbing Everest, "Because it is there,"[19] showcases the potential of the Achiever's strength.

If you possess the strength of the Achiever, you likely love your to-do lists. Every day presents new opportunities to accomplish new things. You take satisfaction in being busy and look forward

---

19: Often attributed to Edmund Hillary, who climbed Everest in 1953. Mallory was the one who first said this, before his fated attempt in 1924.

to being productive in the hours ahead. Your internal drive to finish helps you focus on completing what you started.

You are a doer. The more things you can achieve, the happier and more satisfied you will be.

ACTIVATOR

When Mark Twain said, "The secret of getting ahead is getting started," he was reminding us that not taking action will result in missed opportunities. Activators love to be a part of things at the outset.

If this sounds like you, you make things happen by quickly turning thoughts into action. You are always seeking opportunities to move forward and you excel in determining the best course of action. Your bias for acting, not thinking, makes you willing to take the risk to start something that hasn't been proven.

When you sense your momentum slowing, use your Activator to get going again. Then dial it back a bit. Activator is a great strength to have in reserve.

ADAPTABILITY

Some people are just better than the rest of us at playing whatever cards they are dealt in life. They live in the moment, love spontaneity, and thrive on variety. They accept interruptions and detours. They adapt to them with ease and can see the new opportunities they present.

If this describes you, you thrive in fluid environments and adapt easily to changing demands. You live in the here and now and are comfortable with shifting situations and priorities.

In times of chaos or confusion, your flexibility helps you find opportunities to be productive. You can quickly survey a changing landscape and make the decisions that will lead to the best action right now.

ARRANGER

Imagine the maestro on his rostrum, the director of the big-budget movie, and the ringleader of the circus. In complex dynamic situations, they can identify the optimal outcome by considering all the variables and available resources.

If this sounds like you, you see patterns and are always looking for the perfect configuration of resources to turn confusion into clarity. You evaluate the alternatives, devise new options, and discover the paths of least resistance. As you go about assembling the pieces of the puzzles in your life, the big pictures and the ways forward will emerge.

COMMAND

Whoever says "When the going gets tough, the tough get going" is one who, in uncertain times, can step in, take control of a situation, and make decisions. His Command strength enables him to take charge.

If this describes you, you are comfortable making decisions and leading others. You bring control and order to situations and enjoy being in the driver's seat. You know when to go through a barrier rather than go around it. Your strong presence inspires confidence in others.

Exhibiting Command can bring clarity to ambiguous situations. Because you are undeterred by obstacles and don't shy away from conflict, you can be a persuasive presence. Your courage and decisiveness enable others to be less distracted and to join the common effort.

COMPETITION

Those who are "in it to win it" are invigorated by competing. With no interest in participant ribbons, they thrive on winning.

If this sounds like you, you are intensely aware of others' performance and measure your progress against theirs. Competition involves two parties striving for a goal that cannot be shared.

Find a way to have a small win every day. Try to do something better than someone who is a worthy opponent. If you can compete, you can win. If you can win, you can celebrate.

CONSISTENCY

When Thomas Jefferson began the Declaration of Independence with, "We hold these truths to be self-evident, that all men are created equal," he introduced the guiding hand of constancy into a time of uncertainty. In his efforts to create a stable and predictable society, he believed people function best when rules are clear and fair for everyone.

If this sounds like you, you are keenly aware of the need to treat everyone equally. You know rules keep us safe and the playing field must be level. You are able to make decisions that are the most fair and equitable for all. Doing so, your predictability aids stability. As a result, people see you as trustworthy.

DELIBERATIVE

John Heywood's quote "Haste makes waste,"[20] reminds us how being thorough can help us be more productive.

If you are a careful person, you think before you act and you execute with caution. You sort through the options, anticipate obstacles, and assess the risks. After thorough consideration of each course of action, you make your decision and proceed with certainty.

20: In his 1546 collection of proverbs

CHAPTER 5 - PERFORMING

As you consider the alternatives, draw upon prior experiences when you accurately anticipated what could go wrong.

Your ability to identify the potential for future mistakes can help you produce high-quality results in a ways that minimize risk.

DISCIPLINE

If you 'plan your work and work your plan', you are one who willingly takes all the steps necessary to reach a goal.

If this describes you, you enjoy routines and structure. You like things to be predictable and planned. You want to accomplish tasks in the most orderly and effective way.

When you identify a desirable destination, create and follow the optimal route to get yourself there. Your Discipline will help you move through each stage of the journey in an efficient and orderly fashion.

FOCUS

When you "keep your eye on the ball," you focus on the tasks at hand, which increases your chance of success.

To achieve your desired outcome, concentrate your attention on the desired result. With Focus, you can stay on the most direct path and avoid distractions.

Use your Focus to concentrate on one task at a time and stick with it until it is complete.

MAXIMIZER

"Good to Great" is the Maximizer motto.

Not content with the status quo, Maximizer is always looking for a better way forward, toward more abundance.

If this sounds like you, you are comfortable setting lofty, but practical, goals. You enjoy discovering ways to improve your efforts to attain the best result.

Use your Maximizer to amplify any desirable aspect of your life. You may enjoy a small frisson of pleasure each time you do so.

RESPONSIBILITY

When Carl Jung said, "You are what you do, not what you say you'll do," he was referring to those who can be counted upon to fulfill the promises they make. When they say they will do something, they mean it.

If this sounds like you, you are diligent, dependable, and always keep your promises. You are conscientious about meeting your obligations and stick with your projects until completion. You have a sense of dedication and you take ownership of your responsibilities. You enjoy keeping the commitments you make to yourself and others. This inspires others to trust you and depend upon you.

Allow your Responsibility to be selective about your commitments. Volunteer only for what is worthy of your efforts and brings some joy into your life.

RESTORATIVE

He who says, "We can fix this" views broken as a temporary state. He brings reassurance, reminding us it's possible to put the pieces back together.

If this sounds like you, you have a drive to make things right again. You can identify the underlying factors that led to the damage.

Engage your Restorative to make the best use of existing resources to refresh any issue in your life in need of some revival.

CHAPTER 6

BELIEVING
Live Your Values

with your Personal Strengths[21]

APPRECIATION OF BEAUTY AND EXCELLENCE

GRATITUDE HOPE

SPIRITUALITY

with your Performance Strengths[22]

BELIEF CONNECTEDNESS

21: from the VIA Institute
22: from Gallup, Inc.

The Believing strengths contribute to our self-awareness, improving our understanding of our core values and needs. These strengths help us practice self-care. They are the ones we use to act upon our beliefs. They are crucial for maintaining our mental, emotional, and physical health.

We'll address each of these six Believing strengths with a look at:

- the signals it sends
- what it feels like
- how to use it

Using these strengths can lead us to the inner peace necessary for genuine happiness.

LIVE YOUR VALUES USING YOUR PERSONAL STRENGTHS

APPRECIATION OF BEAUTY AND EXCELLENCE

When Thomas Aquinas wrote, "One will observe that all things are arranged according to their degrees of beauty and excellence,"[23] he was making the case that beautiful and

---

23: c. 1250. Aquinas was a priest and a philosopher in medieval Italy. In his time, the earth's population was around 400 million—it is almost 8 billion today—and life was a hard and brutish affair for most, with scant opportunities to witness much beauty or excellence.

CHAPTER 6 - BELIEVING

excellent things are superior to those that are not. In his time, around 1250, when beautiful and excellent things were scarce, Aquinas associated them with heaven. Fast forwarding to today, when glimpses of beauty and excellence are more accessible, we correlate them with happiness—our heaven on earth.

If Thomas Aquinas's words resonate with you, it means you experience profound feelings and develop close relationships with concepts, things, experiences, and people that you find beautiful or exceptional. You find joy in admiring the wonders of nature, mathematics and science, the arts, and the characteristics and achievements of others. In their presence, you feel awe and are inspired to make your own contributions to the beauty and excellence of the world.

Use your Appreciation of Beauty and Excellence to bring yourself closer to the ideas, objects, and people that align with your values. Whenever you start feeling mentally or emotionally numb during repetitive tasks, take a break. Go outside for a walk or look out of a different window and appreciate the beauty of everyday life. If you look, you will find it. Once you begin noticing beautiful creations of nature and man, it will become easier to discover new ones every time you repeat the exercise. Recognizing the beauty around you and the excellence of other people can have a refreshing effect.

GRATITUDE

People who appreciate their blessings are always prepared to show gratitude for the good things in the world and what they've been given. By doing so, they catch a glimpse of the strength of Gratitude.

If this describes you, you are thankful for many things in your life: a child's smile, a gorgeous sunset, a kind gift from a friend.

Use your appreciation for what you value to bring yourself joy and be thankful for the wonderful things and people in our world.

HOPE

Whoever first said, "Hope is praying for rain, but faith is bringing an umbrella" was illustrating how the strength of Hope promotes positive expectations that can lead to confident optimism.

If you are hopeful, you have a desire and an expectation good things will happen. Your strength of Hope empowers you to move forward in your life and it supports you emotionally. With hope, your positive attitude carries you through life's minor inconveniences. As a result, you are seldom anxious or depressed.

Use your strength of Hope to persevere when a challenge or opportunity. There will be times when you will be unable to come up with a tidy solution to a dilemma. Let hope come to the rescue. Trust what you believe in, be optimistic, and give the good things in your life a chance to happen by wanting them to happen.

SPIRITUALITY

Do you know people who feel connected to something bigger than themselves? If so, you're fortunate to be acquainted with spiritual individuals. They may have the strength of Spirituality in the traditional religious sense, or they may have it in the more contemporary "deepest meanings and values by which people live"[24] sense.

If you are one of them, your strength of Spirituality supports your feeling that we are all connected by something beyond the known and observable realm. If you are religious, your portals to that dimension may be the Scriptures and the values they espouse. If you believe in a force that unites us all to one another, your door to that dimension may be your own values and beliefs. Whether your preference is one or the other or a combination of both, you feel grounded by unseen things that give your life a sense of purpose.

Use your Spirituality to find your reason for being, and to live your life in a way that gives you the highest sense of purpose and

---

24: Philip Sheldrake, *A Brief History of Spirituality* (Hoboken, NJ: Wiley-Blackwell, 2007); David Ray Griffin, Spirituality and Society (Albany, NY: State University of New York Press, 1988)

the greatest happiness. The word spirituality means different things to different people. The best meaning of it for you is what you *want* it to mean. Whatever your definition, use your strength of Spirituality to see your "place in the grand scheme of things and find meaning in everyday life."[25]

LIVE YOUR VALUES USING YOUR PERFORMANCE STRENGTHS

BELIEF

Those who "do the right thing" possess a sense of right and wrong that drives how they act. These folks have deeply held ideals and can be depended upon to uphold their standards. As they do so, they live according to their values and we view them as dependable and trustworthy.

If this sounds like you, your values and principles give your life meaning and a sense of purpose. Your motivation, drive, and determination come from living your life according to your convictions. The most important aspect of your life is staying true to them.

Your strength of Belief enables you to align what you think and do with your values, your purpose, and your ideals.

25: Ryan M. Niemiec and Robert E. McGrath, *The Power of Character Strengths* (Cincinnati, OH: Via Institute on Character, 2019), 268.

CHAPTER 6 - BELIEVING

CONNECTEDNESS

Those with Connectedness consider fate to be inevitable. They know nothing happens by chance. Like Isaac Newton, they see that for every action, there will be an equal and opposite reaction—and everything is somehow all connected.

If you feel this way, you sense we are each part of a bigger whole. You are fascinated by the links between people, ideas, and events. You can see how the little things in the past and present may significantly influence the future.

Use Connectedness to step back and see the connections that run through everyday circumstances. This sense of coherence enables you to take a broader perspective and see how all the different facets of your life contribute to the unique gem that is you.

PART II

THE COMPETENCIES
These Make You Exceptional

> *Competence is how good you are when there is something to gain.*
>
> – MARK MANSON

In this section, we introduce the Level Up Competencies.

The competency movement began in the 1970s with the studies of David McClelland, a Harvard psychology professor. He argued that intelligence tests lacked validity, and that grades did not predict success in real life. He proposed these traditional forms of assessment be abandoned and replaced with a better methodology, which he labeled "competencies." He defined *competencies* as:

> *The underlying characteristics of people, which enables them to deliver superior performance in a...situation.*

If the concept of competencies is newish to you, you may be asking,

WHY COMPETENCIES?

Aren't our strengths enough?

One of the great things about our strengths is that they are multidirectional. They can go anywhere at any time. Their bags are always packed.

But how do we engage our strengths to help us accomplish something specific?

That's what competencies are for.

> *Competencies serve as the conduits to precisely focus our strengths and energies on a desired result.*

As our strengths describe HOW we can think, feel, and act, our competencies describe WHAT we can do with them.

To illustrate, let's imagine some situations where you use only a strength versus engaging a strength to support a competency.

PART II - THE COMPETENCIES

Situation	Only a strength	A competency-strength combo
Social Gathering	*Social Intelligence* Walk in the room, assess the feelings and motives of others.	*Build Productive Relationships- Social Intelligence* Consider the traits and qualities of another who you would like to know better before you engage him in conversation. Use your Social Intelligence to lay a foundation upon which you can begin the relationship.
Start a project	*Analytical* Consider all potential ingredients	*Develop Plans-Analytical* Carefully compare the best potential ways to plan your project.
Rapid Change	*Bravery* Meet the change head on.	*Communicating-Bravery* Let others know you share their concern for the challenges ahead and that you are committed to finding the best possible approach to each one.

We are more effective when we use our strengths to support our competencies. Can you see how the competency focuses a strength to achieve your desired result?

This is why, as adults, it's usually better to be defined by what we can do well, our competencies, than to be announced by general areas in which we have potential, our strengths.

FROM COMPETENT TO CAPABLE

With the Level Up Method, we use our competencies as vehicles to carry our strengths toward the specific results we desire.

Our competencies give us the means to translate our plans into action, achieve favorable results, and improve our capabilities. Who doesn't want to be considered capable? But what is the difference between being competent and being capable?

Competency	The ability to perform at high levels
Capability	The capacity to use competencies in creative and useful ways in new situations

PART II - THE COMPETENCIES

Another comparison:

Competence is an essential ingredient of being capable.[26]

The Level Up Competencies are the ones most useful to living the life you desire.

There are five categories of competencies and 17 distinct competencies within the five categories.

The Five Categories of Competencies

PLANNING
CHANGING
COLLABORATING
ACCOMPLISHING
IMPROVING

Strengths alone are not always enough to help us thrive in our lives. But when used to enhance a valuable competency, our strengths can empower us to achieve desirable outcomes.

Applying our strengths to our competencies, we become more capable.

26: R. Nagarajan and R. Prabhu, "Competence and Capability—A New Look," International Journal of Management Reviews 6, no. 6 (June 6, 2015): 7–11.

As we investigate each competency in the coming chapters, consider how your signature personal and performance strengths can best support it.

As you harness your strengths to improve your competencies, you will be on your way to developing a better, happier you.

For each of the 17 competencies, we will give examples of how you might use a personal strength, or a performance strength, to improve the competency. Note that each strength is featured only once in these illustrations. The strengths that are best suited for you, and that you consider to be the most robust, will be the ones that will aid in improving your competency.

Every segment of the arts, sciences, business, and athletics has its own subset of competencies—the ones that best support achievements in a specific area. Our list of competencies is a collection of the most general ones we use to thrive in our lives.

Here now, are the competencies...

PART II - THE COMPETENCIES

THE 17 COMPETENCIES IN THEIR 5 CATEGORIES

1. **Thinking**
   - Creating Vision
   - Making Decisions
   - Developing Plans

2. **Changing**
   - Tolerating Risk
   - Negotiating
   - Communicating Clearly

3. **Collaborating**
   - Building Productive Relationships
   - Inspiring Others
   - Developing Others
   - Influencing Others
   - Leading Others
   - Managing Conflict

4. **Accomplishing**
   - Taking Initiative
   - Executing Efficiently

5. **Improving**
   - Continually Learning
   - Acting Professionally
   - Continuously Evolving

THE STRENGTH-COMPETENCY-HAPPINESS MODEL

This graphic illustrates how Competencies focus and drive our Strengths toward desired outcomes. By doing so, we attain a sense of Fulfillment that leads to Happiness.

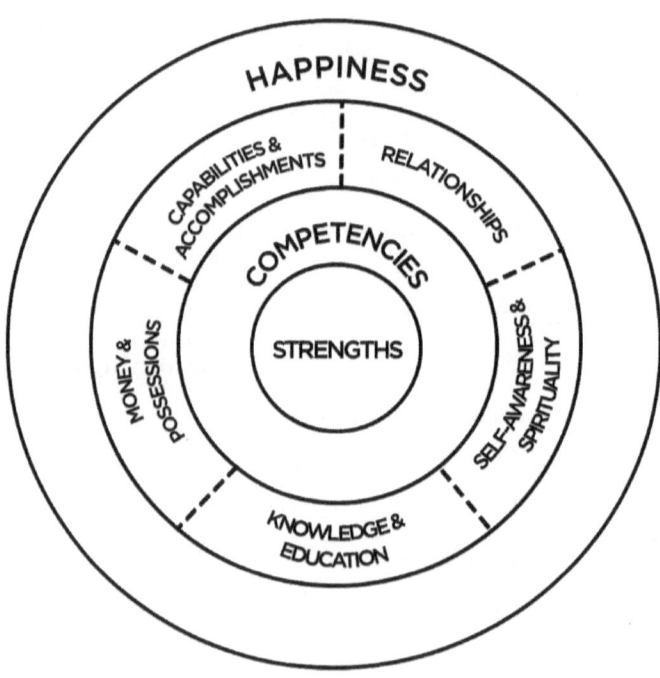

We work *in to out*, using our strengths to support the competencies best suited to propel us toward our highest potential. As we do so, we collect rewarding experiences and produce a variety of outcomes which help us close the Gap.

As we begin to thrive and gain a sense of fulfillment, we are on our way to the best reward of a life well lived–happiness.

Others see us from *out to in*, first noticing how we thrive in our lives. If they wish to better understand us, they might speculate about the competencies we use to live a fulfilling life. If they know us well, they may be able to perceive a few of the signature strengths we regularly engage.

In Level Up, we primarily refer to improving our capability to live up to our potential. Here we capture this in five Fulfillment categories: Education & Knowledge, Capabilities & Accomplishments, Money & Possessions, Relationships, and Self-Awareness & Spirituality.

If this were a physical model with rotating rings, in the central Strengths section would be a pizza of your most robust strengths. The next ring would have 17 sections, one for each competency. By rotating the Competencies ring and the Fulfillment ring, you could "dial in" and align the best competency-strength combo for thinking or doing something that will bring you a sense of fulfillment.

SOME CLARITY ON COMPETENCIES

You may be wondering, "Why are we investing so much in developing our competencies?"

The frank answer is, "Because competent people live more rewarding lives than incompetent ones."

Fortunately, applying nearly *any* strength to *any* competency will result in improved capability.

This means, regardless of your signature strengths, you can develop many competencies with them, using what you've got to get where you want to go.

In fact, using the strengths you have developed to become more competent is downright enjoyable. More on this soon, when we get to the passage on flow.

As your competencies improve and increase in number, so will your self-confidence. Confidence is a key ingredient of living a rewarding life. Having confidence promotes a sense of optimism and calm within and sets the stage for happiness to enter.

COMPETENCY-STRENGTHS COMBOS: YOUR GATEWAY TO FLOW

As you begin to apply your strengths to competencies, you will notice the most effective combinations are the ones that feel most natural and pleasant to use. They are your go-to combos and you own them. When you use these competency-strength combinations, you feel energized and focused. Time stands still; nothing else seems to matter. Thanks to Hungarian-American psychologist Mihaly Csikszentmihalyi,[27] there is a name for this phenomenon—*flow*.

27: "CHICK-sent-me-high-ee"

When we are in flow, he observed, we are in a state of complete concentration and absorption in an activity. And "we're most likely to enter that state of total ...immersion when the challenge of the task is roughly equal to our ability to complete it."[28]

In flow, we are in the zone. Here's a great account from Bill Russell, legendary center for the Boston Celtics:[29]

> *It was almost as if we were playing in slow motion. During those spells I could almost sense how the next play would develop and where the next shot would be taken.*

All of us want to maximize the likelihood of flow in our lives. How to do so? Select and use the C-S combos that feel most natural and *you* will be in the zone.

How to know when we are in a state of flow? It feels like this:

1 Completely involved in what we are doing—focused, concentrated
2 A sense of ecstasy—being outside everyday reality
3 Great inner clarity—knowing what needs to be done and how well we are doing
4 Knowing the activity is doable—that our skills are adequate to the task

---

28: Mihaly Csikszentmihalyi, *Flow: The Psychology of Optimal Experience*, (New York: Harper Perennial Modern Classics, 2008).
29: William F. Russell, *Second Wind: The Memoirs of an Opinionated Man* (New York: Simon & Shuster, 1991).

5   A sense of serenity—no worries about oneself and a feeling of growing beyond the boundaries of the ego
6   Timelessness—thoroughly focused on the present, hours seem to pass by in minutes
7   Intrinsic motivation—whatever produces flow becomes its own reward[30]

THE COMPETENCY-FLOW-HAPPINESS LINK

Can you think of instances when you were in flow—when you knew what to do, did it, and the time flew by? You may not have been aware of it at the time, but chances are you were engaging the C-S combos that felt most natural to you. And you were happy. Csikszentmihalyi discovered that the happiest people are the ones who spend the most time in flow, when they sense forward momentum in their lives. He also found that happiness is an activity, not a fixed state, and can be developed as we learn to achieve flow in our lives.

Your understanding of your unique strengths prepared you for the next step—to select the competencies that will help you thrive in your life. Each of the following five chapters are devoted to a category of competency and the specific competencies within the category.

Now, let's explore how you can develop the competencies that will give your life a sense of flow.

30: Mihaly Csikszentmihalyi, "Flow: The Secret to Happiness," TED Talk, 2004.

CHAPTER 7

PLANNING

Have the Will and Intention to Do Something

Hope is not a strategy.

- VINCE LOMBARDI

(Using our) Strengths is a strategy.

- GALLUP

CREATING VISION
MAKING DECISIONS
DEVELOPING PLANS

When you improve your competencies within the Planning category of competencies, you are beginning to shape a desirable and attainable future.

Planning is the critical first step in preparing to be a better version of you. This is where you evaluate your options and form a program that will take you where you want to go. Planning is an intentional act. It is about being *proactive*, which is creating the future you wish, rather than being *reactive* where you respond to what life hands you and hope for the best.

Planning sets the stage for you to *act.* The three Planning competencies lay the foundation for the competency categories which follow: Changing, Collaborating, Accomplishing, and Improving.

In this chapter, we'll examine each of the three Planning competencies and provide suggestions on:

- What the competency is
- Why this competency is valuable
- What the competency looks like in action
- How to use your strengths to improve this competency in a way that is uniquely suited to you

CREATING VISION

The only thing worse than being blind is having sight but no vision.

—HELEN KELLER

Your vision is the mental image of what you can and want to be.

When you were a child, your vision was what you wanted to be when you grew up.

CHAPTER 7 - PLANNING

Maybe you wanted to ride horses. Or have fancy parties. Or cure cancer. Or celebrate your Nobel Prize for curing cancer while riding your pony at a lavish party. You probably played games or read books that made your vision feel more real to you.

As adults, we have adjusted and refined the dreams of our youth. Still, our mental image of what we can and want to be gives us a sense of destination. We use it to stay focused on our dreams and act with intention.

Your vision is the ideal future state, where you are using your strengths and competencies to realize your aspirations. Can you state your vision in a way that captures your yearnings and inspires you to act? If so, this can help you move your life forward with more enjoyment.

Here are two very different sample vision statements:

> *To laugh often and much; To win the respect of intelligent people and the affection of children; To earn the appreciation of honest critics and endure the betrayal of false friends; To appreciate beauty, to find the best in others; To leave the world a bit better, whether by a healthy child, a garden patch, or a redeemed social condition; To know even one life has breathed easier because you have lived.*
>
> **- RALPH WALDO EMERSON**

To create a better everyday life for the many people.

– IKEA

Our vision carries us emotionally and pushes us mentally and physically to the next level. We can bring our vision to life by engaging our strengths to make it so.

The following are examples of how the personal strength Perspective and the performance strengths Arranger and Futuristic might be useful when Creating Vision.

CREATING VISION WITH YOUR PERSONAL STRENGTHS

PERSPECTIVE

Whatever signature strengths you use when forming your personal vision, invite your Perspective to join the exercise. Perspective, the strength, sees what can be best for the task at hand by considering what is relevant to the situation. Perspective enables the creation of a vision by focusing on opportunities and challenges, rather than being limited by artificial boundaries or distracting details.

Use your Perspective to extend the dimensions of your vision, bringing it breadth and depth.

CHAPTER 7 - PLANNING

CREATING VISION WITH YOUR PERFORMANCE STRENGTHS

ARRANGER

In others' vision statements, we often see broad categories presented in the order of their importance to the author. Emerson's above is a superb example of this approach.

How did he align the cars in his vision train to be in precisely the order he intended? It sure looks like one of his signature strengths was Arranger. Keeping a lot of things in your head and placing them in the most logical structure comes naturally to Arranger.

FUTURISTIC

By applying the Futuristic strength to the Creating Vision competency, one can imagine a world where many things become possible. Use your Futuristic strength to create a vision which energizes and inspires you.

Your Futuristic strength can also help you consider how your other strengths might participate in the journey to your desired future state—your vision.

MAKING DECISIONS

The most difficult thing is the decision to act, the rest is merely tenacity.

– AMELIA EARHART

After creating a vision, our first step toward realizing it is to decide how to proceed.

Making Decisions is the competency that helps you find the way forward when you are faced with ambiguity and uncertainty.

The competency of Making Decisions is presented in the Planning category as a bridge between Creating a Vision and Developing the Plans to realize it.

Our Five Step Decision-Making Process and the Eisenhower Matrix are two tools which will help you consider the key issues in your life and how to make better decisions.

CHAPTER 7 - PLANNING

FIVE STEP DECISION-MAKING PROCESS

1 Identify an issue and why it is important.
- What is the potential for gain if you address it?
- What is the potential for loss if you ignore it? What competency-strength combos can you use to define its potential impact?

2 Gather the information needed to solve the problem.
- What facts will be needed?
- What competency-strength combos could you use to investigate the issues?

3 Determine what your options are.
- What approaches should be considered; who will be affected; is time a factor?
- What competency-strength combos will help you compare different approaches?

4 Evaluate the alternatives.
- What are the benefits and risks associated with each course of action?
- What competency-strength combos will help you assess each one?

5 Select the best course of action.
- Is it one for which you can form feasible plans?
- Which competency-strength combos will help you make your decision?

Use the Five Steps as a framework into which you can insert your unique contributions—your knowledge, your experiences, and your intuition. As you do so, you will sense your judgement improving.

The Five Steps + Your Judgement = Good Decisions

When you use your good judgement in a solid decision-making process, you will have earned the right to trust the decisions you make.

THE EISENHOWER MATRIX

There are several ways to make decisions well, and many ways to make decisions badly. We often look to historical figures who were able to make decisions in key moments and study how they made them when the stakes were high and the choices felt limited.

Dwight D. Eisenhower served as the Allied Forces Supreme Commander during WWII, as NATO's first Supreme Commander after the war, and as the 34th President of the United States from 1953 until 1961. This latter period is the time referred to as the Cold War, when the nuclear arms race between Russia and the United States was marked by the mutually assured destruction of both countries if either side launched a nuclear attack. This was the pervasive theme of life in the middle of the last century.

Can you imagine the pressure on Eisenhower to make countless important decisions in rapid succession for many years? He made thousands of life-or-death calls, relying mostly on his judgement, without the benefit of computers. With millions of people depending on him, how did he do it? One answer may be found in his point-of-view.

> *What is important is seldom urgent, and what is urgent is seldom important.*

When he had a choice, he spent his time thinking about and doing what he regarded as important, but not urgent.

Here is a version of Ike's simple decision-making model:

THE EISENHOWER MATRIX

	URGENT	NOT URGENT
IMPORTANT	**Q1** **DO** *it now* - Emergencies - Deadlines - Demands from above	**Q2** **SCHEDULE** *a time to do it.* - Planning & Learning - Relationships & Family - Exercise & Rest
NOT IMPORTANT	**Q3** **DELEGATE** *it to someone else* - Unnecessary meetings - Doesn't achieve your goal - Technical issues	**Q4** **ELIMINATE** *Stop doing this* - Voluntary distractions - Busy work - Gossip & Worry

His simple grid model served him well in times of crisis. By choosing to focus on the *Important but Not Urgent* tasks first, he led our country through a time of uncertainty and anxiety.

While we may not have Eisenhower's strengths and competencies, we can improve our Making Decisions competency by applying his model to determine which undertakings will be most fulfilling and worthy of our attention.

Here are examples of how the personal strengths Judgement and Prudence, and the performance strengths Analytical, Ideation, Achiever, and Context might be used when Making Decisions.

MAKING DECISIONS WITH YOUR PERSONAL STRENGTHS

JUDGEMENT

Judgement, the strength that weighs all the evidence before drawing a conclusion, is the linchpin of solid decisions. How stable can a decision be without the benefit of good Judgement?

To improve your Judgement, converse with others you respect on topics that matter to you. Religion and politics excluded, people usually have nuanced views on most issues. Whether their views differ a little or a lot from yours, they may inform how you consider an issue. As you do so, you will strengthen your Judgement.

Use your Judgement to examine other alternatives. Select the best ones and you will make solid decisions.

PRUDENCE

One with Prudence is careful about choices and doesn't make decisions that necessitate taking undue risk.

If you sense you're rushing into decisions, Prudence can help you slow down, reflect, and carefully consider each element before making your decision. By taking this momentary pause, Prudence will help you consider all the facts and make a well-thought-out decision.

Use your Prudence to reduce distractions and filter out unusable suggestions to Act Now! With Prudence, you can remain focused on making decisions that will best serve you and others in the future.

MAKING DECISIONS WITH YOUR PERFORMANCE STRENGTHS

ANALYTICAL

Analytical is an objective problem solver and makes decisions based on the evidence. This quality makes Analytical a desirable addition to any decision-making process.

Using Analytical to reveal what lies beneath the surface of issues in your life will enable you to make informed decisions about your plans.

IDEATION

Do any two Planning strengths have less in common than Ideation and Analytical? Probably not, but Ideation can broaden our perspective when Making Decisions.

Ideation is the strength with the lightbulb over his head. When we want new ideas, we need Ideation to get things going. Connect the dots in new ways.

Suggestion: A few nights before making a big decision, take Analytical and Ideation out for drinks. Then leave. As the label on fireworks says, light the fuse and run. Let them get to know each other. They may discover all kinds of fascinating things about what the other can bring to the process. And you will benefit from their interplay and the wide range of contributions they bring to your decision-making.

CHAPTER 7 - PLANNING

DEVELOPING PLANS

A goal without a plan is just a wish.

– ANTOINE DE SAINT-EXUPÉRY

Developing Plans is the process of laying the most direct path to reach the most desirable destination. Planning helps you set goals and prepares you to wisely use your resources to achieve the intended results within a specified time.

Award for Best Definition of Planning goes to Alan Lakein:

Planning is bringing the future into the present so that you can do something about it now.

How good is that? It's so good that Amazon sells a laser-cut 8x10 wooden plaque of it. A must-have for you planners.

By Developing Plans, we mean Developing *Achievable* Plans. Almost anyone can develop a plan.

What's the difference between a plan and an achievable plan?

An achievable plan is one which embraces the use of your signature strengths and the appropriate competencies to produce a desired result. Applying your competency-strength combos to realize a plan greatly improves the odds you will achieve the best possible outcome.

While we're handing out awards, here's the winning entry for Best Reason Why Planning Is Important:

> *If you fail to plan, you are planning to fail.*
>
> – BENJAMIN FRANKLIN

Developing Plans, "bringing the future into the present so you can do something about it now," isn't a perfect process. No matter how much we plan, the future will remain mysterious. What actions can be taken when the vision is solid but the strategy to achieve it isn't working? Take a step back, pause, and pivot—maintain your vision, but reevaluate, adapt, and refine the plan. Consider which new competency-strength combos will be best suited to help you realize the new plan and you'll be on your way again.

Here are examples of how the personal strength Creativity and the performance strengths Input and Strategic can make contributions when you are Developing Plans.

CHAPTER 7 - PLANNING

DEVELOPING PLANS WITH YOUR PERSONAL STRENGTHS

CREATIVITY

Developing Plans involves finding new ways to complete existing tasks or tackle new challenges. Creativity can discover the most effective methods for developing practical strategies.

Creativity works at every level. Use your Creativity from the bottom up to help you find new practical solutions to everyday problems. And use it from the top down to help you think differently about the best way to approach big issues.

DEVELOPING PLANS WITH YOUR PERFORMANCE STRENGTHS

INPUT

Inquisitive by nature, Input always wants to know more. Any planning project is better with Input and the library of knowledge he brings.

Use your Input to acquire a broad assortment of information that could be useful to consider before you create your plan.

STRATEGIC

Strategic, seeing the big picture, can add stability and durability to the planning process.

When Developing Plans, Strategic can envision the most efficient way to use what you've got to get where you want to go. Few other strengths are as good as Strategic *before* the planning begins, helping you consider what to include and what to exclude in your plans.

CHAPTER 8

CHANGING

Welcome What's Next

When you're finished changing,
you're finished.

– BENJAMIN FRANKLIN

TOLERATING RISK
NEGOTIATING
COMMUNICATING CLEARLY

Changing is the process of becoming different, making the transition from the present to the future. Change can be driven by you or by others. Your participation in change driven by others may be voluntary or involuntary. The change you experience may be gradual or sudden; partial or radical; positive, negative, or neutral. Here we see how the Level Up Method can help you navigate the changes you experience in your life.

Think of the change process as:

Present State → Transition State → Future State

Change is born and educated in the present state, lives in the transition state, and retires in the future state.

Your Changing competencies will help you bring intentionality to the process of transitioning from the present to the future. With them, you will use your strengths to understand and tolerate the risks and resolve issues along the way.

Perhaps the best reason to change intentionally:

> *If you do not change direction, you may end up where you are heading.*
>
> —LAO TZU, 450 BC

(Did Lao Tzu just make an early reference to The Gap?!)

Next best reason to change intentionally:

> *If you don't like change, you're going to like irrelevance a lot less.*
>
> —TOM FELTENSTEIN

CHAPTER 8 - CHANGING

Myth in need of busting: "Change is bad."

Change is *not* bad, change is...life. Imagine an unchanging you, frozen in time, motionless. You don't want that, do you? Well, maybe a couple weeks lying on a sun-kissed beach after a grueling cold winter might be a nice...change.

To help us ready our strengths to support our Changing competencies, let's examine the nature of change and how it affects us.

WHAT CAUSES CHANGE?

The changes we experience are commonly driven by a mixture of external and internal factors.

THE MAIN EXTERNAL CAUSE OF CHANGE

A New Environment

Our world tomorrow will be different from our world today. The forecast is for:

Changes in our Surroundings. The area around us is constantly in motion. Weather, travel, and politics will always provide variety.

People change. Our relationships with others shift as they come into or leave our lives.

Health changes. When it's good, we often take it for granted. When it turns, we may feel we have a new adversary in our lives.

Things change. Available housing, means of transportation, the selection in the supermarket, and our sense of financial security fluctuate throughout our lives.

<u>The two internal drivers of change</u>

Approach

You want more of something or someone. Money, friends, shiny things, knowledge, success, and serenity come to mind. Leading consequence of #1 New Year's resolution in the approach category: new gym memberships.

Avoidance

Any *bête noire*—something or someone you want less of. Debt, illness, and anything or anyone that annoys you lead this category. Leading consequence of #1 New Year's resolution in the avoidance category: sales of diet books.

CHAPTER 8 - CHANGING

INTERNAL OBSTACLES TO CHANGE

*Whatever you are not changing,
you are choosing.*

- LAURIE BUCHANAN

What keeps us from navigating the changes deserving of our attention? A leader in the study of change cites:

Three Barriers to Change[31]

1. Failure to See
2. Failure to Move
3. Failure to Finish

What better to help us avoid these pitfalls than our strengths? How about:

Barrier	Personal Strength	Performance Strength
1 Failure to See	Perspective	Futuristic
2 Failure to Move	Bravery	Activator
3 Failure to Finish	Perseverance	Achiever

31: J. Stewart Black, *It Starts with One: Changing Individuals Changes Organizations* (Hoboken, NJ: Pearson Publishing, 2013).

WHAT ARE THE TYPES OF CHANGE?

Most changes are one of two primary types:

Proactive Change — Anticipating the need for change and getting out in front of it. Every time you take the initiative to refine your approach to something, you originate a change.

Reactive Change — Responding to signs that changes are needed. Most lie somewhere between the CHANGE ENGINE OIL light on your dash and a total power outage.

Windows of opportunity open and close. How can you position yourself to be near them when they open so you can participate in the first type of change? When gold nuggets were first found in a California river, which was the better choice:

A. To be one of the 300,000 miners; or
B. To make durable trousers for the miners, as Levi Strauss did?

CHAPTER 8 - CHANGING

WHAT ARE THE CHARACTERISTICS OF CHANGE?

The four types of challenges presented by change are captured in the acronym VUCA.

Volatile	Rapid, sudden change	Earthquake
Uncertain	Unclear information and outcomes	Clear air turbulence
Complex	Multiple variables and unknowns	Election
Ambiguous	Lack of clarity about the meaning of events	Traffic jam

Each VUCA challenge requires its own response. All evade predictability and clear cause-and-effect links. Each Changing competency—Tolerating Risk, Negotiating, and Communicating Clearly—will give you an opportunity to use different strengths to reduce the VUCA in your life.

Examples of strengths you might use to navigate different challenges presented during change:

VUCA	Personal Strength	Performance Strength	to–
Volatility	Self-Regulation	Self-Assurance	Promote stability
Uncertainty	Perspective	Analytical	Reduce unpredictability
Complexity	Judgement	Arranger	Diminish the # of choices
Ambiguity	Creativity	Ideation	Find new ways to adapt

Are you ready to handle some of the changes in your own life? Using your competency-strength combos will help boost your competence and confidence. In times of change, you will have an inner excitement as you face new challenges, and an outer calmness that will inspire and motivate others.

Now, let's investigate the Navigating Change competencies: Tolerating Risk, Negotiating, and Communicating Clearly.

Keep these in the top tray of your competency toolbox for when, despite all your expert planning, life becomes uncertain. For each of these, here are a few observations on what it is, why it's important, what it looks like in action, and how to use your strengths to improve it.

CHAPTER 8 - CHANGING

TOLERATING RISK

Only those who will risk going too far can possibly find out how far one can go.

– T. S. ELIOT

Every player in every sport has a ready stance. Picture the elite tennis player just before the ball is served to him, light on his feet and ready to spring in any direction.

He's prepared to take the risk that comes with the opportunity to perform.

In times of change, Tolerating Risk is your ready position. Use it to stay light on *your* feet.

Why is Tolerating Risk so helpful to us? Because understanding risks and choosing which ones to take can put us on the path to dramatically improve things in our lives. Times of change often present significant opportunities to improve our situation. Can you bear another sports metaphor? Think of making personal progress as would a surfer. The ability to increase velocity greatly improves the opportunity to catch a wave. Very few of us are surfers, but all of us can catch waves of change in our lives.

The first step in Tolerating Risk is understanding risk. When you know the potential for gain or loss, how often it may occur, and what impact it might have, you can make decisions about what to do with it.

The way we approach change, and the risks that come with it, is a blend of our personal level of risk tolerance and the potential impact the change will have on us. Some of us are natural risk takers, big wave surfers; some of us are risk averse, happy paddling around in the bay on a foam board; most of us are somewhere in the middle, skewing one direction or the other depending on the circumstances and who's watching.

Did you notice our competency is Tolerating Risk, not Conquering Risk? Conquering Risk would make a fine competency for the Roman god who slays risk. But we are not gods. As humans, our best approach is to try to understand the change around us, to be watchful for opportunities it brings, to influence it when we can, and to see it through. As such, Tolerating Risk is not a one-size-fits-all competency. Tolerating Risk means staying in our ready position throughout phases of change. Here are three approaches that will help you boost your ability to tolerate the risks which accompany the changes in your life.

CHAPTER 8 - CHANGING

3 WAYS TO IMPROVE YOUR ABILITY TO TOLERATE RISK

1. Stay Flexible
2. Manage Your Expectations
3. Remain Resilient

How do you accomplish each of these? With your strengths! Let's see how.

STAY FLEXIBLE

The easiest way to change something is to change your viewpoint.

– HARRY PALMER

The appropriateness and effectiveness of our strengths and our competencies varies depending on the context in which they are used.

Our ability to create and use different competency-strength combos is particularly useful during periods of change.

For example, during times of change, the social climate around you may shift. Consider which strengths will become more useful and which strengths will be less suitable when the atmosphere switches from:

Relaxed	to	Formal
Playful	to	Serious
Boisterous	to	Quiet
Optimistic	to	Wary
Thinking	to	Feeling

Will you use different strengths as the conditions change? Of course.

MANAGE YOUR EXPECTATIONS

I always love to be careful with my expectations so that life has pleasant surprises for me.

– SEBASTIAN THRUN

During times of uncertainty, expectations are the things considered most likely to happen.

The classic advice to manage the expectations of others is to under-promise and over-deliver. But how do we manage our self-expectations?

Assigning ourselves unrealistically high expectations has two predictable results: burnout and speed-related incidents, such as train wrecks.

But we also know that low expectations will not propel us toward our potential.

A nice approach to improving your Tolerating Risk competency is to manage your expectations to the right level, assigning yourself what Daniel Pink calls "Goldilocks tasks." These are challenges that are not too hot and not too cold, neither overly difficult nor overly simple."[32]

Let's say you want to get in better shape. Examples of Goldilocks tasks would *not* be "Watch someone else do a pushup," or "Sign up for twenty consecutive days of CrossFit classes." But they might include "Walk around the block every day," or "Get an evaluation from a fitness coach."

REMAIN RESILIENT

It's not that I'm so smart, it's just that I stay with problems longer.

– ALBERT EINSTEIN

During periods of change, we encounter all sorts of difficulties. Resilience is the capacity to recover from difficulties.

32: Daniel H. Pink, *Drive*, (New York: Penguin Random House, 2009), 118.

With your Tolerating Risk competency, you will be able to handle the inevitable setbacks that will accompany even the best-laid plans. Using your strengths to tolerate risk will help you navigate both expected and unexpected changes.

Depending on your perspective, the risks associated with Changing can be exhilarating or frightening. People who enjoy a mix of fright and excitement find intense amusement park rides exhilarating. The rest of us are happy on the carousel. Or watching the carousel.

Wherever you are during change, when the ground begins to move, hold on to your signature strengths to comfort and steady yourself.

Remember, this too shall pass.

Now let's see how the personal strength Bravery and the performance strengths Adaptability and Positivity can help us tolerate risk.

CHAPTER 8 - CHANGING

TOLERATING RISK WITH YOUR PERSONAL STRENGTHS

BRAVERY

Those with Bravery may appear to be fearless. More likely, they consider their vulnerabilities and uncertainties just as the rest of us do. Then they act.

Bravery is the courage to confront uncertainty and handle it to the best of your ability in order to keep moving forward in your life. When you engage your strength of Bravery, it can enable you to tolerate risks and tackle them with productive thoughts and actions.

TOLERATING RISK WITH YOUR PERFORMANCE STRENGTHS

ADAPTABILITY

In sports, a utility player is able to play several different positions competently. During times of change, Adaptability is our go-to utility player. Adaptability's ability to stay in the present and shift approaches enables him to make rapid adjustments in fluid times.

Consider the preflight briefing message: "In the event of a sudden loss of cabin pressure, put your mask on first before helping others." Thankfully, this rarely happens. When it does, who do you think is the first to take that action? You guessed it—Adaptability. By accepting risk, one can act quickly during a time of sudden change.

POSITIVITY

Changing is hard. If there is one kind of person to particularly avoid during times of change, it is the negative person. Notice that negativity is not a strength.

Are you familiar with the story of Chicken Little? Chicken Little throws his farmyard into a panic by proclaiming that "the sky is falling!" Versions of this ancient oral European folktale date back many centuries. Don't let a Chicken Little inject chaos into your farmyard by framing the change you are navigating as the beginning of the end. If he wants to play the victim, let him do so elsewhere.

Positivity can be your best friend during times of uncertainty.

An optimist, Positivity neither welcomes nor shuns risk. When risk presents itself, and morphs into change, Positivity stays cheery. She chooses to look on the bright side. If she is nearby, her very presence will help you better Tolerate Risk.

When Changing, you may experience many emotions. Being down is one of them. When that time comes, don't sink; let Positivity throw you a life ring. A bit of positivity will help you see what is right rather than what is wrong with the situation and give you the resilience you need to get back on track. Positivity, like the coast guard, rescues those who swim towards it. When you feel a bit down, look for Positivity.

NEGOTIATING

Negotiating is the process of settling your differences with another person or group to move forward in your life. The goal of negotiating is to reach an agreement while avoiding an argument.

During times of change, many things may be in motion at once—your projects, other people, your surroundings, even the rules. To stay or adjust your intended course during change, when external forces are trying to pull you elsewhere, can involve a lot of bargaining along the way.

Negotiating is another of our free-range competencies, good in a variety of situations. It is especially valuable to have during times of change.

ZOPA, WIFE OF ZORRO?

When using your Negotiating competency, your first goal is to reach a Zone of Possible Agreement, or ZOPA. Also called the bargaining range, this is the place where potential agreement will benefit both sides more than the alternative options. Outside the zone, no amount of negotiation will yield an agreement.

You're coming from the left; the other side is coming from the right. The place where you overlap? That's the ZOPA.

Use your strengths to move into a zone of possible agreement and broaden what you can consider a win, from a point to a range, and give yourself more room for an acceptable outcome.

CHAPTER 8 - CHANGING

THE 4 STAGES OF NEGOTIATING

To achieve your best result, use different strengths throughout the negotiating process. Notice how the strengths shown below can be helpful during each of the four stages of negotiating.

Stages of Negotiating	*Personal Strengths*	*Performance Strengths*
1 Preparation	Perspective	Strategic
2 Exchanging Information	Love of Learning	Communication
3 Bargaining	Creativity	Maximizer
4 Closing and Commitment	Perseverance	Achiever

Are you feeling better prepared to use your Negotiating competency during times of change? You have the tools you need—your strengths and the roadmap of the stages of negotiating. Use these to plan your approach and obtain a beneficial result for yourself.

Now let's see how the personal strength Perseverance and the performance strengths Communication and Self-Assurance might come in handy when Negotiating.

NEGOTIATING WITH YOUR PERSONAL STRENGTHS

PERSEVERANCE

Negotiating can be difficult. This does not mean it cannot be an enjoyable and informative process on the way to producing results. Most oft-cited reasons why negotiating is difficult include the demands on the participants to be persistent, overcome obstacles, and finish what they started. Know who can be persistent, overcome obstacles, and finish what they start? One with Perseverance!

When negotiating, Perseverance sticks with it. This may come more naturally to him than it does to the rest of us, but he still has to work at it. He prepares by organizing himself so he will be able to remain in the negotiations until they are finished.

NEGOTIATING WITH YOUR PERFORMANCE STRENGTHS

COMMUNICATION

Let's invite Communication, the most free-range strength, to help us negotiate.

CHAPTER 8 - CHANGING

Every stage of Negotiating, from preparation to commitment, benefits from communicating precisely. Use Communication at the front end to gain clarity during preparation. Use it at the back end to confirm the agreement at the closing and commitment stage.

SELF-ASSURANCE

A valuable asset to have during any negotiating process is confidence. Without it, the other side, sensing weakness, may pounce. With Self-Assurance, you don't have to be aggressive or even assertive. Self-Assurance lets everyone know you are comfortable in a negotiating role, will address issues as they appear, will represent the interests of your side, and will see the negotiations through to an acceptable result.

The other side, sensing Self-Assurance's comfort with risk, will be less inclined to try tactics to destabilize you.

You know Changing can be hard. Negotiating during change can be really hard. Having Self-Assurance and your "I can do this" attitude can help keep your mood buoyant when the details of negotiating are trying to pull you down.

COMMUNICATING CLEARLY

Communicating is not about speaking what we think. Communicating is about ensuring others hear what we mean.

– SIMON SINEK

Communicating and sharing information with others can be achieved through speaking, writing, or using body language.

Communicating Clearly is highly useful at enhancing many of our other competencies. It is included in Changing because communicating openly, honestly, accurately, and deeply is crucial to achieving the best result during times of change.

Here are a few examples of how your personal and performance strengths can be used when you are the sender or the receiver during communications about change.

CHAPTER 8 - CHANGING

When sending a message, engage your:

Personal Strength	*Performance. Strength*	*to convey:*
Perspective	Connectedness	What is happening now is just part of life
Prudence	Deliberative	I'm being very careful with this change
Zest	Futuristic	Think of what tomorrow might bring
Creativity	Ideation	This is a chance to consider new ways forward
Kindness	Includer	This will benefit many
Hope	Positivity	This change will help improve things
Honesty	Responsibility	I am going to do what I promised
Bravery	Self-Assurance	This *will* work

When receiving a message, engage your–

Personal Strength	Performance. Strength	to understand:
Judgement	Analytical	What is being communicated
Social Intelligence	Empathy	Where the sender is coming from
Curiosity	Input	What new concepts are being introduced
Love of Learning	Learner	Opportunities for personal growth
Zest	Positivity	The beneficial aspects of the change

Communicating throughout change is essential. And if we skip over communicating at any stage, it will make the following stages more difficult. Are you familiar with The Rule of Seven? The Rule of Seven states that people need to hear something seven times before they understand and warm to it.

CHAPTER 8 - CHANGING

Get out in front of the change, and communicate early and often before it becomes too complex to convey. When it comes to the frequency and methods you use to communicate change, more is better.

Now let's see how the personal strength of Humor and two very different performance strengths, Command and Empathy, can be useful when Communicating Clearly during change.

COMMUNICATING CLEARLY WITH YOUR PERSONAL STRENGTHS

HUMOR

When Mark Twain said, "Humor is the good-natured side of a truth," he was observing that a bit of levity can make the facts of a matter more pleasant. By not being unnecessarily serious, those with the strength of Humor have a positive and gentle outlook on life.

Some things *are* deadly serious. But if we have our health and a sense of security, true threats account for a fraction of what is in our lives.

For everything else, why not enjoy our time here as best we can? If you can use your strength of Humor to do so, your positive emotions will help to decrease your anxiety and the nervousness of those around you.

COMMUNICATING CLEARLY WITH YOUR PERFORMANCE STRENGTHS

COMMAND

Command is a rare bird in the strengths aviary. In peaceful times, we may be able to get along with other strengths as proxies for the presence it brings. In times of change, Command's steadying influence can be exactly what is needed to deliver us through the storm.

Command doesn't have to be at the podium in a fancy suit to be effective during times of change. Think of George Washington, how he respected and cared for his soldiers at Valley Forge during the severe winter of 1777–78. Surrounded by the enemy in freezing weather, their clothes in tatters and their bellies empty, the soldiers subsisted, and later thrived, on the comfort they received from his visits, his concern, and his Command. He was out there with them throughout that cold winter, communicating by doing, walking the talk. We owe Washington, his Command, and those soldiers a lot.

When the going gets tough, Command is comfortable taking charge. The way he communicates brings order and control to change and inspires confidence in others. During times of uncertainty, everyone can use a little more of the confidence that Command brings.

CHAPTER 8 - CHANGING

EMPATHY

When the change coin flips, it comes up either as an opportunity or as a threat. During fluid times, the coin flips often. We already know what to do with opportunities: seize them.

What about threats? During periods of change, Empathy is a welcome addition to any gathering. Empathy is a beautiful strength to have when the environment is changing and people feel uncertain about what is to come.

CHAPTER 9

COLLABORATING

Work with Others on Common Goals

If you want to lift yourself up, lift up someone else.

– BOOKER T. WASHINGTON

THE COLLABORATING COMPETENCIES

BUILDING PRODUCTIVE RELATIONSHIPS
INSPIRING OTHERS
DEVELOPING OTHERS
INFLUENCING OTHERS
LEADING OTHERS
MANAGING CONFLICT

Collaborating is examining and accomplishing desirable things with other people. The competencies in this category each provide a valuable ingredient to collaborating––momentum.

Without momentum, collaborating can come to a halt quickly. Worse, it may reverse.

BUILDING PRODUCTIVE RELATIONSHIPS

Nobody cares how much you know, until they know how much you care.

– THEODORE ROOSEVELT

Building Collaborative Relationships is developing positive connections with others and cooperating with them as you attain a common objective.

When we have strong collaborative relationships with those around us, life is more enjoyable and we are more productive.

Building Productive Relationships is a big competency, one that takes time to develop. Our competencies are bundles of abilities, knowledge, and skills. A few in the bundle of Building Productive Relationships are listening, understanding, communicating, being generous with your time, encouraging others, assisting others, compromising, keeping promises, demonstrating empathy, being open, and being patient. Thankfully, we don't have to do all these at the same time.

The thing people most look for in others is a sense of *connection*. For thousands of years, we used hugs, rubbing noses, and handshakes to connect with one another. Then came the introduction of mail, the telephone, and the internet.

Every interaction with people is a chance to use our strengths, to build relationships, and collaborate. New opportunities to connect with others often present themselves at intermediate-sized gatherings: social events, group meetings, and participating in sports.

Now, let's see how the personal strengths of Honesty and Love and the performance strengths Harmony and Relator can contribute to Building Collaborative Relationships.

BUILDING PRODUCTIVE RELATIONSHIPS WITH YOUR PERSONAL STRENGTHS

HONESTY

When parties are sincere in their thoughts and deeds, they lay the foundation upon which deep relationships can be formed. Honesty, the strength that exemplifies truth and sincerity, is one that can help promote building collaborative relationships of the most durable kind.

Those with Honesty among their signature strengths are viewed as the steadier and more authentic among us. They can be depended on to honor their commitments and not take shortcuts that will compromise what they believe in.

If you wish to build a collaborative relationship with someone, keep your Honesty at the forefront early in the relationship.

LOVE

Those who exhibit the strength of Love show us they value their close relations with others. Love, the personal strength, includes our general love for people and our deepest affectionate feelings for others. Those with Love among their strengths often use it to contribute to the formation of collaborative relationships that are reciprocal and valued by both parties.

Use your strength of Love to show others you appreciate your collaborative relationships with them. A few ways to do so are by displaying tolerance, empathy, and forgiveness when you are with them.

CHAPTER 9 - COLLABORATING

BUILDING PRODUCTIVE RELATIONSHIPS WITH YOUR PERFORMANCE STRENGTHS

HARMONY

When building relationships, first impressions matter. A lot. Members of the American Society of Pessimists, if there were such a thing, might be intrigued by the contrariness of a new acquaintance. For the rest of us, agreeability gets the relationship ball rolling. No other strength has the capacity for agreeability the way Harmony does.

When you have a potential new relationship in sight, bring your Harmony into the conversation. It works great one-on-one and is highly effective when meeting people in a group. Use your Harmony to deliver geniality to any gathering.

Use Harmony to seize opportunities for building new relationships, enhancing relationships between others, and being a collaborative partner.

RELATOR

Relator goes deep. And she sees other Relators as people like us. When we first meet a person with a signature Relator, we may perceive her as a bit distant. Nothing could be further from the truth. Relator is one with whom you can build a lasting relationship.

Relator is a strength which brings trust to relationships. Some people create relationships easily, only to see them inexplicably dissolve just as quickly as they were formed. Relators, with their interest in strong mutual partnerships, have a natural ability to find common ground on which genuine connections can be based. Relators are trusted and valued collaboration partners.

INSPIRING OTHERS

Our chief want is someone who will inspire us to be what we know we could be.

– RALPH WALDO EMERSON

Inspiring Others is the competency which demonstrates you believe in yourself and others.

Inspiring Others promotes an atmosphere of positive emotional energy and encourages others to do their best work.

Consider Ernest Hemingway's "Courage is grace under pressure." When people see you stay your course under strong headwinds, you inspire them. When the winds blow you backwards for a while, as they will occasionally, others will be heartened by your persistence.

CHAPTER 9 - COLLABORATING

What are some qualities of those you find inspirational? Chances are they include helping others feel valued, which gives rise to their sense of optimism and purpose.

Here are some ways to use our strengths when Inspiring Others:

Personal Strengths	*Professional. Strengths*	*To inspire others by giving them:*
Love	Achiever	encouragement to reach their potential
Fairness	Consistency	assurance that they will be treated fairly
Social Intel	Empathy	the feeling that they are understood
Perseverance	Focus	an appreciation that you will see this through with them
Curiosity	Futuristic	excitement about where we are headed
Love	Includer	the message that they are welcome
Creativity	Ideation	fascination for what is possible
Zest	Maximizer	optimism that we are going from good to great

Can you see the multiplier effect Inspiring Others has? Every time you use this competency, at least two people benefit immediately.

INSPIRING OTHERS WITH YOUR PERSONAL STRENGTHS

FORGIVENESS

One of the most moving experiences is seeing one in a position of influence give another person a second chance. Watching Forgiveness in action, we are inspired by the character of the forgiver.

Those with the strength of Forgiveness don't feel burdened to carry the memory of every disappointing act of others into the future. They can shake them off and get on with their lives. And they can give those who have let them down another opportunity to show their merit and value. Most of us have behaved badly at one time or another. We have those with Forgiveness to thank that these instances are not the ones that define us. And those who exhibit their Forgiveness can also inspire us to be more lenient with others in the future.

If you find yourself upset by something someone important to you has done, confide in a person whose signature strengths includes Forgiveness and let her help you navigate through your emotions. She may help you realize that the other person's good deeds outweigh this recent transgression and that forgiveness is possible.

GRATITUDE

Have you ever been inspired by someone telling you they feel blessed? This lucky soul is also telling us something else—she enjoys feeling grateful as she goes through life.

Most of us find happy people inspiring. Where do they get their happiness? Maybe from this link:

Gratitude → Satisfaction → Happiness

When we feel and act grateful, we experience greater satisfaction. The more satisfied we are, the happier we are. The happier we are, the happier others are. The happier others are, the more inspired they become.

When you sense someone isn't feeling satisfied with his life, bring your strength of Gratitude into the conversation. We all have a bit of "monkey see, monkey do" in us, which is the natural tendency to mirror the emotions and actions of others. When you express Gratitude in your life, your enabling words may inspire him to feel his own.

HUMILITY

When people with the strength Humility demonstrate that others should be recognized before them, we feel inspired. When the awards for being wonderful are passed out, they prefer to receive theirs last.

Use your strength of Humility to let others know you want to lift them up and celebrate their contributions. They, sensing your healthy self-esteem and regard for their place in the grand scheme of things, will feel drawn to and inspired by you.

INSPIRING OTHERS WITH YOUR PERFORMANCE STRENGTHS

CONNECTEDNESS

Connectedness, the strength, knows we are all part of something larger than ourselves. The competency of Inspiring Others involves confidently demonstrating faith and trust in yourself and others.

Those with Connectedness have a conviction things happen for a reason and everything is part of a bigger picture. When Connectedness lets others know *they* are also in that picture, it has a calming effect. People feel more certain about their relationships, more optimistic about collaborating, and inspired by Connectedness's assurance that we are all in the same boat.

CHAPTER 9 - COLLABORATING

Using your Connectedness to build and strengthen your relationships helps others feel less vulnerable in the face of unpredictability. Your confidence is inspiring and stimulates others. What better gift to bring into a relationship than a boost to the other person's confidence? Your Connectedness can help you do this.

INCLUDER

Includer wants everyone to be on the inside. When you let others know they are part of your world—your goals, your successes, and your celebrations—they feel a lift. Your interest and support inspire them.

Includer is not seeking homogeneity. Includer is fine with differences in people and perspectives. When others sense this, they feel accepted. The sense of safety that inclusion provides encourages people. They feel energized and confident when all are welcome.

Life can be chaotic. Includer dampens a common effect of chaos—when people feel they are becoming untethered from their community. Includer says, "No, you're right here with us, just like everyone else." Includer is very good at Inspiring Others during times of uncertainty.

CONSISTENCY

Consistency is keenly aware of the importance of treating all people the same. With its innate sense of fairness, it has a steadying effect on others, helping them be less anxious and more receptive.

When people feel uncertain about their environment, their inspiration is at its lowest point. A cause of uncertainty in social groups or professional organizations can be the perception of favoritism. Whether real or imagined, when people feel others are getting a better deal than they are for no good reason, their morale plummets. It takes with it their ability to be inspired. A temporary approach to Inspiring Others may be whipping them into a lather with overenthusiasm. A more durable approach to Inspiring Others is to consistently act in ways which create a sense of stability and assure them of fair treatment.

Consistency, with its quiet and deep sense of equality, has a calming effect on others as it helps them feel more inspired about their prospects.

CHAPTER 9 - COLLABORATING

DEVELOPING OTHERS

The greatest good you can do for another is not just to share your riches but to reveal to him his own.

– BENJAMIN DISRAELI

Collaborating, the category of competencies, enables us to make a difference in the lives of others in a variety of ways.

The competency Developing Others involves demonstrating our care for people and our willingness to assist them. As we develop others, we encourage and empower them to make progress on the issues that matter most to them. When we choose to develop others, we can make a big difference in their lives.

Developing Others deepens your relationships with them and increases their sense of potential. When you turn your attention to helping others improve, everyone benefits. The recipients of your efforts appreciate the support and the sense of forward motion you bring them. As Developing Others promotes talent acceleration, their morale and productivity will improve.

Helping others develop brings us a satisfaction. This thought from Dorie Clark captures it perfectly:

Once you've achieved your own goals, the next—profoundly fulfilling—step is to help teach others how to achieve theirs.[33]

When others are aware of your belief that everyone deserves a chance to reach their full potential, it will create an environment where they feel empowered to thrive.

People don't like to be over-instructed in prescriptive programs.

> *Grass doesn't grow faster if you pull on it.*
>
> – AFRICAN PROVERB

Use the Level Up Method to enable another's voyage of discovery to be more interesting and fulfilling.

Developing Others is the "children are our future" of the competencies. Let's see how the personal strength Kindness and two performance strengths, Individualization and Maximizer, can help us aid others in living their best lives.

33: Dorie Clark, *Stand Out* (New York: Penguin Random House, 2015).

CHAPTER 9 - COLLABORATING

DEVELOPING OTHERS WITH YOUR PERSONAL STRENGTHS

KINDNESS

Developing others begins with your decision to help them grow and moves quickly to how you express it to them—as a question, a suggestion, or an offer. One who shows Kindness when developing others lets them know he is concerned for their well-being and truly wishes them the best.

Expressing your Kindness when developing others gives them a sense of safety during their process of improvement. A world with more kindness in it is a better world. Also, as a bonus, people who demonstrate Kindness feel better. When you do something for another, don't you get a little lift? That's your complimentary shot of endorphins, which are released when we are generous to others. The effect this has on us is coined "the helper's high."

DEVELOPING OTHERS WITH YOUR PERFORMANCE STRENGTHS

INDIVIDUALIZATION

Those who have someone with Individualization to actively engage in their development are truly fortunate. Individualization, the strength that sees the unique qualities of each person, can dial in to what makes people special and how they might use what they've got to get where they want to go.

Have you ever seen plate spinners at the circus? They try to spin as many plates as they can on top of poles without dropping the plates. The spinner pays keen attention to each plate, darting back and forth to attend to the ones that need more momentum. Individualization is like that when Developing Others. Intrigued by the unique qualities and requirements of each person, Individualization can give them what they most need when they need it. By the way, the record for the most plates spun simultaneously is 108. It took a lot of Individualization to do that!

Use your Individualization when Developing Others. Let them know you see their unique characteristics and you believe in their potential. Then offer them whatever resources they need to stay in motion and move forward.

CHAPTER 9 - COLLABORATING

MAXIMIZER

Maximizer is the good-to-great strength. Maximizer doesn't go anywhere near fixing weaknesses.

Use your Maximizer to bring optimism and a sense of self-worth to others as you help them develop. Your Maximizer sees the potential in them and will set the bar at a height you know they can clear so they can achieve their new personal best.

As you engage your Maximizer when Developing Others, your encouragement will give them a lift and help them live more fulfilling lives. With your support, they can resign their Flat Earth Society memberships because now there are so many new places they can go.

INFLUENCING OTHERS

> *The people who influence you are the people who believe in you.*
>
> – HENRY DRUMMOND

Influencing Others is the competency that indirectly shifts how people think and act. The purpose of influencing others is to help them improve their chances of producing positive outcomes.

The three preceding Collaborating competencies have prepared you to now improve and make use of your *Influencing Others* competency.

> *Building Collaborative Relationships*, you connected others to you. People prefer to be influenced by those they know and trust.
>
> *Inspiring Others*, you gave them optimism. To be influenced, people first need to feel inspired.
>
> *Developing Others*, you helped them improve their ability to succeed. As people experience your interest in their improvement, they sense compassion and are encouraged to use their new capabilities to think and do new things.

As you demonstrate these competencies, you will have an energizing effect on others.

Other people can't directly motivate us. We have to do that for ourselves. But others can influence us. This powerful adage describes the relationship between motivation and influence:

> *Motivation gets you going.*
> *Influence is what makes you go in a particular direction.*

Think of the people who are influential in your life. What do they have in common? The first thing that usually comes to mind is that they are confident. Does their confidence come from competence? Probably. Another thing we notice about influential people is they know what they are talking about. They've done their homework. And they can read their audience. They often know a lot about the people who are important to their lives because they took the time to build relationships with them. When people demonstrate these attributes, we perceive them as trustworthy and we are influenced by them.

Let's see how our personal strength, Social Intelligence, and our performance strength, Significance, may be used to Influence Others.

INFLUENCING OTHERS WITH YOUR PERSONAL STRENGTHS

SOCIAL INTELLIGENCE

The first step in influencing others is gaining their trust.

We feel those who understand why we are the way we are "get us." When they do, we perceive them as more deserving of our trust. And we are far more likely to be influenced by those we trust than by those we don't.

INFLUENCING OTHERS WITH YOUR PERFORMANCE STRENGTHS

SIGNIFICANCE

Significance, a rare strength, is not one we often witness. Residing in the Enabling set of strengths, it is well suited to help us influence others.

Significance, determined to do what it can to make the world a better place, also encourages others to reach for the stars. Because Significance is goal oriented, it avoids unimportant tasks. When it does so, others are influenced to also focus on the essential and create an impact of their own.

Significance is stimulating to be around and very good at Influencing Others.

LEADING OTHERS

All of us are smarter than any of us.

— DOUGLAS MERRILL

Two or more people working together to achieve a common goal make a team. Your team, whether you are the leader or a member, is your tribe. You and the other members of your tribe

CHAPTER 9 - COLLABORATING

use your unique abilities to make progress toward a common goal.

Leading Others means providing them the guidance, direction, and encouragement to achieve their desired results.

Why is Leading Others important?

> *Never doubt that a small group of thoughtful committed citizens can change the world; indeed, it is the only thing that ever has.*
>
> – MARGARET MEAD, CULTURAL ANTHROPOLOGIST

Working together gives people a sense of belonging, purpose, and accomplishment.

By Leading Others, you assist them in establishing meaningful connections and striving together towards shared goals. Working as a member of a team gives them a sense of identity.

Let's see how the personal strength Teamwork and the performance strengths Competition and Arranger can be used to lead others.

LEADING OTHERS WITH YOUR PERSONAL STRENGTHS

TEAMWORK

Teamwork, the strength that enables us to be loyal contributors, is a desirable one for any team member. For our leaders, it is a mandatory one. Because if a leader is not working for the common good, he must be working to benefit himself. When team members sense their leader isn't a team player, they might become disenchanted and withdraw from the team.

When you are Leading Others with your Teamwork strength, you feel a connectedness to the team and a deep engagement with the work of the team. As your team members recognize this, they become more willing and eager to follow your lead. When you share the responsibility for getting the work done, they feel you are one of them. For example, baseball coaches wear the team uniform and behave as if they are members of the team, and football coaches often dress like the fans. If someone knows why basketball coaches wear jackets and ties, please explain it to me.

Leading Others, use your Teamwork strength to be someone others can depend upon as an active leader of the team. As you do, it will promote respect for your leadership and a willingness to work with you in the future.

CHAPTER 9 - COLLABORATING

LEADING OTHERS WITH YOUR PERFORMANCE STRENGTHS

COMPETITION

What do Competition and Leading Others have in common? They both love winning! Competition invigorates us to do our best to beat our rivals.

For those with Competition among their signature strengths, success is measured not by excellence, but by how well they perform against an opponent seeking the same result.

Competition keeps one eye on the prize and the other on the opposition. It measures progress frequently and is quick to respond with a course correction when it will help his collaborators succeed.

ARRANGER

Arranger is the strength that can identify optimal blends of resources and people to achieve a desired result. Arranger looks for, and can see, the effects different approaches will produce.

The common goal team collaborators share is to fulfill their shared purpose.

Who can effectively align each party's role in a collaboration with where they can make the greatest impact? Arranger.

Unassigned or, worse, mis-assigned collaborators can be like loose cannons on the deck of a ship in a storm, casting about and smashing into each other. Thoughtfully assigned, they bring a sense of order to any collaborative effort.

MANAGING CONFLICT

Peace is not the absence of conflict, it is the ability to handle conflict by peaceful means.

– RONALD REAGAN

Conflict occurs when two or more parties with different perspectives compete for the same resources. Examples include territory, food, water, and the hearts and minds of others.

When Collaborating, there will often be some conflict between individuals or groups. Unresolved conflict dampens productivity and carries with it a heavy load of unnecessary expenses, such as time lost, being unproductive, wasted resources, emotional toil, and the costs of lost opportunities.

Managing Conflict is the process of identifying and reducing disputes. Benefits of Managing Conflict include replacing this

CHAPTER 9 - COLLABORATING

impediment to progress with an understanding of what led to the conflict and improved relationships going forward.

The purpose of Managing Conflict is to find the places where the collaborating parties can agree on how to work together. When each appreciates the other's special qualities and challenges, they are more capable of finding ways their differences can work for them rather than against them.

THE POTENTIAL FOR CONFLICT

The potential for conflict arises when

- The journey of a person coming from one place and going to another intersects the journey of a person coming from somewhere else and going to a different destination. Midair collision.
- Two people are coming from and going to the same place and one person gets in the other's lane. Someone cut in your line.
- Two people coming from different places are trying to get to the same place. Fistfight at the oasis.

The primitive choices for ending conflict were fight, flight, fake, or fold.

Fight   Win-lose
Flight   Run away
Fake   Pretend to play dead
Fold   Okay, have it your way

A better option is:

Find   How to use our strengths to manage the conflict

FIVE STEPS TO MANAGE CONFLICT

Try this straightforward strengths-based approach to improve your Managing Conflict competency:

1. Are both sides willing to end the conflict?
2. Find common ground, a shared goal acceptable to both sides.
3. Name each side's objectives to achieve their goal. Often, this is where the conflict lives.
4. Name the strengths each can use to achieve their objective.
5. What will it look like when the conflict is resolved?

The loftiest goal of managing conflict: Collaboration.

When both parties in a conflict acknowledge each other's strengths, they can discover new ways to collaborate and reduce the likelihood of future conflicts.

CHAPTER 9 - COLLABORATING

Caveat: Not all conflicts can be resolved.

Some people are just wired in such a way that they annoy you. If your differences are of a superficial or cultural nature, try to overlook them. If your differences stem from opposing values, there may not be much either side can do about it. Just agree to stay out of each other's way when you can.

■

Okay, I think you've got this. You now have an uncomplicated Five Step strengths-based framework to manage conflict. You're not looking for conflict, but when it does come knocking, you'll be ready.

Now let's see how the personal strength Fairness and the performance strengths Communication and Individualization can be useful when Managing Conflict.

MANAGING CONFLICT WITH YOUR PERSONAL STRENGTHS

FAIRNESS

Those with the strength of Fairness, capable of making decisions objectively without preference for their own feelings and opinions, have a talent for managing conflict. As they see the conflict from the outside-in, they exhibit respect for all parties and can promote compromise where it will serve to lessen or resolve the conflict.

Use your Fairness strength to give each party in a conflict, including yourself, the same chance to express his position. When you don't play favorites, others sense the outcome will be an equitable one.

MANAGING CONFLICT WITH YOUR PERFORMANCE STRENGTHS

COMMUNICATION

Communication, the strength of transmitting messages accurately and convincingly, is valuable to have on your side when you are Managing Conflict. Think of Communication as the lubricant that can unstick conflict.

With its ability to provide the exchange of accurate information between two parties, the Communication strength greatly benefits Managing Conflict. There is a name for this: shuttle diplomacy. Shuttle diplomacy, alternating your attention between two disagreeing parties, takes a lot of effort. It is mentally challenging, labor intensive, and stressful, but it's a very effective way to promote resolution of a conflict.

Managing Conflict-Communication is a great competency-strength combo.

CHAPTER 9 - COLLABORATING

INDIVIDUALIZATION

Individualization appreciates the unique characteristics of people. Comfortable with the differences between them, Individualization can personalize relationships with others to bring out the best in them.

Use your Individualization when Managing Conflict to acknowledge the contributions of the other party. When you do this, they will feel better understood. Less defensive, they will begin to understand the contributions and strengths of the other party. When this happens, you will have used your Individualization to bring the conflict to an inflection point—a change in the shape of the trajectory. When the opposing side feels understood by their opponent, they will relax their positions and gain an interest in resolving the issue.

When Individualization helps open the door of mutual understanding even a sliver, the end of disagreement begins. Trust then forms and a willingness to reach resolution will follow.

All this is thanks to Individualization coming to the rescue of Managing Conflicts.

CHAPTER 10

ACCOMPLISHING

Finish What You Start

Some people want it to happen, some wish it would happen, others make it happen.

– MICHAEL JORDAN

THE ACCOMPLISHING COMPETENCIES

TAKING INITIATIVE
EXECUTING EFFICIENTLY

Results are the outcomes brought about by actions.

Accomplishing is the category of competencies we employ to implement our plan, guide the process, and produce the outcomes that serve our intentions.

Accomplishing things gives us forward momentum. Without direction and intentional action, nothing will happen in our lives except fortuitous events. Taking Initiative and Executing Efficiently, we are the opposite of opportunists, those who only act when they perceive a way to take advantage of a situation.

Every competency up to this point has prepared us for this moment. Now it's time for us to act with intent and enthusiasm.

TAKING INITIATIVE

If there is no wind, row.

– LATIN PROVERB

Taking Initiative is beginning a task or a plan of action toward a result you desire.

Even with a solid strategy and the resources to see it through, starting something can be hard. To take initiative in a new way or on a new thing is not easy. It is especially challenging when you have neither momentum nor something to build on. It's perfectly natural to feel your big bang will fizzle. Except yours won't, because you have your competency-strength combos to make it happen.

A valuable feature of Taking Initiative is that it provides one last chance for reflecting on the competencies and strengths you will consider before acting. A few opportunities for Taking Initiative:

Occurrence	*Your Action*
Something breaks	Find a way to fix it
A new obstacle presents itself	Back your plan up a few steps to see the way over, around, or through.
A new opportunity presents itself	Consider your most natural way to seize it

Extra points if you thought about some strengths which could help you do these things!

Taking Initiative is not a place where we will want to spend a lot of time. It is a waypoint, a spot where we can revisit our plan and gather our focus before we act. Two simple steps will prepare and enable you to take initiative: consider your motivation and remove potential barriers to action.

FIRST, CONSIDER YOUR MOTIVATION...

Like the actor who asks the director, "What's my motivation here?" exploring *why* you are doing something before you act will inform you how to play your role. Understanding what you want to achieve and why you want to achieve it will help you choose which strengths to call upon to produce the desired effect. Periodically reminding yourself of what first motivated you will help you act in the ways most beneficial to achieving the results you desire.

Reflect a bit on the source of your motivation. Is it intrinsic or extrinsic?

Intrinsic motivation arises from within and produces a desire to do something that will be personally fulfilling. Those who are intrinsically motivated often cite their pursuit of excellence or happiness. The things you do just because you want to are those you are motivated intrinsically to do. You willingly, often eagerly, prepare yourself—studying and practicing—to engage in these activities. The result may be personal growth, a sense of accomplishment, or simply enjoyment. What does Taking Initiative look like when it is the response to intrinsic motivation? For example, let's say you want to write a short story for your own amusement. You may:

1. Ponder a few subjects and pick one.
2. Consider from what point-of-view you will write.
3. Check out how-to websites and books, and examples of this kind of writing.
4. Join a writers' group for support.
5. Pick the personal resources you will use to write the story.
6. Sit down to a blank screen or a sheet of paper.
7. Begin writing.

Look at all the steps you took on the way to starting your story. Question: Where could you say you were Taking Initiative?

CHAPTER 10 - ACCOMPLISHING

Answer: At every step until the final one.

At the point when you put pen to paper or tapped the first keystroke, you were Executing. Efficiently, we assume. Because you planned well and took initiative, you were *prepared* to act.

Extrinsic motivation comes from outside us. Potential for reward or punishment are common extrinsic motivators. So much of life is extrinsically motivated. Children attend school because their parents expect them to. Adults work to provide food and shelter necessary for themselves and their families. Some people do things just to test themselves against others.

The child in class, the runner in the race, the worker on the assembly line, and the chess player in the tournament—all measured against their peers—are extrinsically motivated.

On the path to your vision, you will encounter both intrinsic and extrinsic motivators.

Question: Which type is preferable?

Answer: Whichever kind gives you the best opportunity to use and enjoy your signature strengths as you make progress.

Intellectuals tend to be intrinsically motivated. Professional athletes deeply understand extrinsic motivation. The rest of us are somewhere in between, depending on the opportunities available and how we define success.

...THEN, REMOVE BARRIERS TO ACTION

You've considered, studied, reviewed, and pondered the big issues. You developed a plan. Yet something is keeping you from moving to GO.

You are still "fixin' to get ready." It's time to address and clean up those lingering barriers to Taking Initiative.

Common barriers include:

- Conflicting priorities: Resolve them now. Quickly. They had their chance.
- Too many choices: Narrow them down to three, then one. The time for thinking was the past. Now is the time for doing. Two most often cited reasons for inaction are too many choices and self-doubt.
- Distractions: Put them on hold. If they hang up, you can call them back. Or not.
- Fear of Failure: With your strengths and competencies—not even possible!

When you've reconsidered your motivation and removed barriers to action, you're ready to take initiative. Here's a little encouragement from someone who is comfortable with literally starting with a blank page:[34]

---

[34]: No planning, story arcs, and plot development for Stephen King. He just starts writing. Really.

CHAPTER 10 - ACCOMPLISHING

You can, you should, and if you're brave enough to start, you will.

– STEPHEN KING

Now let's consider how the personal strengths Hope and Leadership and two very different performance strengths, Activator and Restorative can be beneficial when Taking Initiative.

TAKING INITIATIVE WITH YOUR PERSONAL STRENGTHS

HOPE

In my seventh-grade catechism class, I was assigned this motto:

Faith is the assurance of things hoped for, the conviction of things not seen.

– HEBREWS 11:1

I had no idea what it meant. Maybe that's why it was given to me, or maybe because my birthday was 11/1? Today, I know exactly what it means: hope and faith are inextricably linked.

Hope, the strength that gives us positive expectations for what may come, encourages us to have faith in the future and take those first steps toward it.

Use your strength of Hope to initiate your actions. Engaging your Hope will promote optimism in yourself and in those around you. When you and others feel optimistic, you believe that what you do will help things turn out well.

LEADERSHIP

Successful leaders don't just mobilize others and induce them to act. They create a vision and organize others in a way which best supports them in working with one another to achieve their shared goals. As they do so, they use their strength of Leadership to take the initiative now that will drive results later.

If this sounds like you and you enjoy taking initiative early and often, volunteer to become a leader!

CHAPTER 10 - ACCOMPLISHING

TAKING INITIATIVE WITH YOUR PERFORMANCE STRENGTHS

ACTIVATOR

Activator, the strength that initiates new thoughts and actions, is a powerful initiator. Activator is always on the lookout for opportunities to do something fresh.

Activator lives in that small space between thinking and acting. Use Activator when Taking Initiative to shorten the time between your thinking and your doing. When you are truly ready, Activator can be the strength to help you start in a new direction.

RESTORATIVE

Things will break. It happens. When they do, you can spend a lot of time investigating the cause and evaluating the options. Even after doing so, it can be difficult to choose the best way to begin the repairs. This is what Restorative does. Restorative loves finding ways to fix what is broken. Restorative can identify what caused a breakdown and initiate a plan to fix it. Restorative knows that broken is a temporary state. Restorative, moving calmly and methodically, can be a fine strength to help you get things back into working order and moving again.

A bit of a stealth strength, Restorative waits calmly for something to break so he can repair it. When we desperately need something to be fixed, Restorative is the one who can assess what must be done and begin the process to set things right.

Here's an example we can all relate to: the customer service rep with a genuine interest in getting our issue resolved and service to us restored. When our credit card is denied, our computer crashes, or our car grinds to a halt on the highway, we tend to panic. How thankful we are when the person on the other end of the line gives us assurance he will resolve our issue. Thank you, Restorative, for Taking Initiative!

EXECUTING EFFICIENTLY

Vision without execution is hallucination.

— THOMAS A. EDISON

Executing Efficiently is the well-prepared you, putting your plans into effect.

Another gem from Edison:

Opportunity is missed by most people because it is dressed in overalls and looks like work.

Success isn't always realistic goal, but doing the work is a very practical aspiration. Happiness from the satisfaction of a job well done is *the result* of doing good work.

Another great quote on Executing Efficiently is this one from Maya Angelou: "Nothing will work unless you do."

So, after all your preparations, how to execute is quite straightforward—work. Can you do the work? You can. That's what your strengths and competencies are for—to help you do the things which will propel your life forward. Soon it will be you saying, *The harder I work, the luckier I get.*

Now let's see how the personal strengths Zest and four performance strengths—Achiever, Deliberative, Focus, and Responsibility—can be used to help us Execute Efficiently.

EXECUTING EFFICIENTLY WITH YOUR PERSONAL STRENGTHS

ZEST

Those with the strength of Zest go about getting stuff done with energy and enthusiasm. They do things wholeheartedly and feel alive and excited by what they can achieve.

When you use your strength of Zest, you can deeply engage yourself in your endeavors. As you do so, you will sense your life is more fulfilling, meaningful, and purposeful.

EXECUTING EFFICIENTLY WITH YOUR PERFORMANCE STRENGTHS

ACHIEVER

Achiever executes. That's what he does. Not one to rest on his laurels, Achiever starts every day at zero and measures his progress at the end of every day.

Who's the one who is already *doing* when the rest of us are just *arriving*? Achiever. And he's happy about it. Even on Monday.

DELIBERATIVE

Unsure which path to take in your life? Engage your Deliberative to carefully evaluate your options. The result will be executing with the certainty that comes from thorough consideration. Contrast Deliberative with Activator:

Activator	Ready-Fire-Aim
Deliberative	Ready-Aim, Aim, Aim-Fire

When you gotta move *now*, Activator is the way to go. When caution is required, go with Deliberative.

FOCUS

Focus, a strength with a long attention span, can help you concentrate on what will help you Execute Efficiently.

We've all witnessed and admired people who perform with little wasted motion, such as the recording studio musician, the cool quarterback, or the smoothly moving student in the tai chi class. They are...focused.

RESPONSIBILITY

Executing Efficiently occurs in three stages: starting, doing, and finishing. Responsibility, the strength of dependability, comes in during the doing, sees it through to finishing, and turns the lights off after everyone else has gone home.

Use Responsibility to be loyal to your obligations and take ownership of your results. As you do, you will execute more efficiently and deliver the outcomes you desire.

CHAPTER 11

IMPROVING

Practice Self-Awareness and Self-Care

Make the most of yourself, for that is all there is of you.

– RALPH WALDO EMERSON

THE IMPROVING COMPETENCIES

CONTINUALLY LEARNING
ACTING PROFESSIONALLY
CONTINOUSLY EVOLVING

Improving is consciously bettering yourself.

In the preceding chapters, we looked *outward,* forming and improving competencies to help us think and act in the ways which are most fulfilling to us. We now look *inward* to three competencies we can use to grow internally. These competencies are just for you.

As we are Improving, we

- Gain new resources to help us move forward.
- Prepare ourselves to become more competent.
- Map our progress.
- Boost our self-awareness and confidence.
- Increase our capacity to close the Gap and Level Up.

Think of Improving as your voluntary and ongoing intervention. To make way for your new ways of thinking and acting, you will need to discard some of the old ones. Another benefit of Improving: For some reason, throwing out old stuff just *feels* good.

A world in which we are all trying to be better versions of ourselves is a good one.

Think of a time when you used some new knowledge or skill to do something better than before. It felt good, right? If we want more of the little pick-me-ups we get from bringing the new into our lives, we need to continue developing ourselves.

As we improve, we experience new accomplishments, increased confidence, and a more meaningful life. Possibly more significant, Improving shrinks the environment where negative stuff can happen. Improving tamps down the potential for stalls and derailments—the two leading causes of malaise and feeling less vital.

Take a moment to consider what might give you a sense of living a more meaningful life. Don't be too hard on yourself; you can always move the bar up later. Moving the bar down is no fun.

Improving is a process, not an act, of developing the competencies of Continually Learning, Acting Professionally, and Continuously Evolving at your own pace one day at a time. This is a good place to remember my grandmother's advice "Life by the inch is a cinch, by the mile is a trial."

CONTINUALLY LEARNING

Chance favors a prepared mind.

- LOUIS PASTEUR

Continually Learning involves acquiring new knowledge and skills to effectively respond to challenges and opportunities.

When we learn, we grow. Continually Learning prepares us to efficiently adapt to the changing demands in our lives.

Unattributable but great aphorisms on learning include: "The more you know, the more you grow." And, even better, "The more you know, the more you know you don't know." Which is not really from Aristotle, no matter what the poster says.

Learning is like going to school, right? Not really. Check out these fine observations by George Couros, a wizard on the subject of learning:[35]

- School promotes starting by looking for answers. Learning promotes starting with questions.
- School is about finding information on something prescribed to you.
- Learning is about exploring your passions and interests.
- Schools teach compliance.
- Learning is about challenging perceived norms.
- School is standardized.(needs square bullet)
- Learning is personal.
- School teaches us to obtain information from certain people.
- Learning promotes that everyone is a teacher, and everyone is a learner.
- School promotes surface-level thinking. Learning is about deep exploration.

Once we progress from credentialed channels of learning, we determine what we'll learn, how we'll learn it, and at what pace. The key to continually learning is to make it a habit. ABL: Always Be Learning. If you do so, you will not only improve your perspectives, you will also discover new occasions to use

---

35: George Couros, "School vs. Learning," The Principle of Change blog, December 27, 2014, https://georgecouros.ca/blog/archives/4974.

CHAPTER 11 - IMPROVING

your strengths and competencies. That right there is the case for Continually Learning.

SEVEN BENEFITS OF CONTINUALLY LEARNING

Continually Learning means making outlays to secure a larger stake in a blue-chip investment: our future selves. In return for the contributions of our time, inquisitiveness, and effort, we receive some nice dividends:

1. New insights and broader perspectives
2. Ability to think more comprehensively
3. Current knowledge of trends that may affect us
4. Better prepared for new challenges
5. Learning new concepts promotes the creation of new ideas
6. Rise in our value, both to ourselves and others. And, saving the best for last,
7. Increased self-confidence

Another benefit of Continually Learning is its amplification of our signature strengths.

Let's see some sample benefits of Continually Learning with the personal strengths Honesty and Spiritualty, and two very different performance strengths, Analytical and Empathetic.

- One with the personal strength Honesty will pursue learning that helps her be more authentic.
- One with the personal strength Spirituality will seek to learn more about how he can connect with his higher purpose.
- One with performance strength Analytical will gravitate to learning that helps him understand a subject more deeply.
- One with the performance strength Empathy will happily immerse herself in new information that helps her better understand others.

Continually Learning—a natural strengths booster.

A casual style of occasional learning, where you pick up pieces of this and that, is okay. But *directional* learning is more likely to achieve the leveling-up you want in your life. A common question is, "How do I determine the curriculum for my life to get me where I want to go?" Try this exercise to reveal topics worthy of your further exploration:

Look:	*To learn something that will help you:*
Inward	Be a better person in some way
Outward	Be of greater value to others
Backward	Remedy a suboptimal capability
Forward	Prepare for the future

There is no "right" way to learn. Investigate any topic between you and your vision of yourself. The inevitable result will be some self-development. The only must-do is ABL...always be learning!

Let's see how the personal strengths Curiosity and Love of Learning and the performance strengths Learner and Context can help us be Continually Learning.

CONTINUALLY LEARNING WITH YOUR PERSONAL STRENGTHS

CURIOSITY

Those with the strength of Curiosity love to acquire new information, new experiences, and new friends. They are open to concepts, activities, and people who offer them opportunities for investigation and inspiration.

Use your strength of Curiosity to support your quest to be continually learning . One way Curiosity can help us learn more about anything or anyone is by starting with "why?"[36]

Have you've heard of the Five Whys? This is an iterative technique asking "why?" five times after each answer to

---

36: If "starting with why" sounds familiar, it may be because you have seen the terrific Simon Sinek TED talk "Start with Why" from 2009. Viewed by 70 million people, it is subtitled in 43 languages

question. It is an effective method to determine the underlying cause of almost any problem. Created by Sakichi Toyoda for his Toyota Motor Company, it is a powerful tool for detectives and children who want some answers. Feed any unresolved issue into your own Five Whys process and prepare to be enlightened.

When you find you are losing interest in something you are trying to do, engage your Curiosity to help you discover why. As you begin to take apart what is behind your sense of disconnection, you may discover new reasons and new ways to reaffirm your commitment to your efforts. Or you may find that you are drifting away from it for good reason. Either way, Curiosity can get you on the path to discovering the answer.

LOVE OF LEARNING

We know the Love of Learning strength naturally supports us in our effort to discover and understand new things. Let's see if we can discover something fresh here.

Continually Learning may be motivated by an external force. In the US, our K-12 education system is funded by state and local governments at the level of a trillion dollars per year, about $17,000 per pupil annually. Compulsory school attendance varies by state. It starts between ages 5 and 7 and continues until ages 16 to 19.

As adults, internal forces are the most common motivators for our Continually Learning. Those with the strength Love of Learning commonly acquire knowledge just for the mental stimulation and pleasure that learning new information brings them. They find joy in acquiring a deeper understandings of things they can use in their everyday lives.

CONTINUALLY LEARNING WITH YOUR PERFORMANCE STRENGTHS

LEARNER

Learner is the strength of inquisitiveness. We can all learn. Learner loves the *process* of acquiring new information. If you have Learner among your signature strengths, you naturally seek opportunities to discover new things. The one with the stack of unread books on his bedside table and a calendar full of webinars? Typical Learner!

For Learner, Continually Learning feels automatic. For the rest of us, we can take inspiration from the zeal with which a Learner dives into the exploration of the new. At an early age, mirroring the behavior of others can be one of the best shortcuts to gain new information and capabilities. Think about how you first learned to throw a ball. Did you read the instructions before you attempted it? Unlikely. You probably watched a kid who knew what he was doing, and then you tried to do it like he did. Eventually, it worked.

As we become adults, we gain the ability to improve by thinking more than by doing. Learners of every age eagerly look for information on how to better think and act.

CONTEXT

Context, drawing lessons from the past, can increase the effectiveness of Continually Learning. Think of Context and Futuristic as bringing different time dimensions to the present. As Futuristic brings the vision of the future to the present, Context brings the lessons from the past to the present:

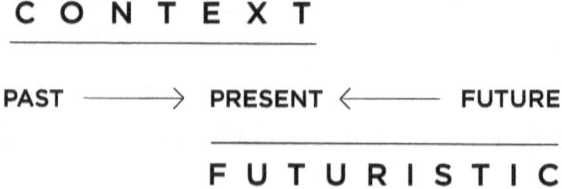

FUTURISTIC

You may have heard Winston Churchill's quote, "Those who fail to learn from history are condemned to repeat it." He was referring to Context. By bringing to the present what we have learned from the past, Context adds an element of efficiency to our learning. Context allows us to start with what is already known, saving us the expenses associated with relearning it.

CHAPTER 11 - IMPROVING

ACTING PROFESSIONALLY

A professional is someone who can do his best work when he doesn't feel like it.

– ALISTAIR COOKE

Acting Professionally means being approachable, resourceful, dependable, and good at what you do. Acting Professionally helps us all level up faster.

THE SEVEN INGREDIENTS OF ACTING PROFESSIONALLY

Here are seven simple ways you can be perceived as Acting Professionally:

1. Be positive
2. Be friendly
3. Be self-aware
4. Live your values
5. Put your strengths and competencies to productive use
6. Do the work
7. Remain resilient

To incrementally boost your professionalism, practice developing these one at a time.

We now explore how the personal strength Self-Regulation and two performance strengths, Belief and Woo, can support our Acting Professionally.

ACTING PROFESSIONALLY WITH YOUR PERSONAL STRENGTHS

SELF-REGULATION

A big part of Acting Professionally is behaving in a controlled and stable manner. Those with the strength of Self-Regulation can think and perform in the measured ways we associate with acting professionally.

Use your strength of Self-Regulation to improve your study habits when you wish to learn new things, your behavior when you wish to convey to others that you are dependable, and your appetites when you need a greater sense of self-control.

CHAPTER 11 - IMPROVING

ACTING PROFESSIONALLY WITH YOUR PERFORMANCE STRENGTHS

BELIEF

Belief, with its keen sense of what is right, is a strength naturally aligned with Acting Professionally.

Those with Belief live in ways which give their lives meaning. They honor their convictions and naturally align their actions to them. When they do so, they exhibit both a sense of commitment to their deeply held principles and the durability to remain true to them.

WOO

Woo, Gallup's acronym for Winning Others Over, launches the Acting Professionally process quickly. Woo, always self-aware, leads with positivity and is sincerely friendly. Woo exudes warmth and professionalism by connecting and showing a genuine interest in others.

Those with Woo love gatherings of all kinds. They will effortlessly meet people, introduce them to one another, and inject energy into the room.

Take another peek above at our Seven Ingredients of Acting Professionally. The opening ones are Positivity, Friendliness, and Self-Awareness. Woo is a marvelous strength with which to exhibit these.

CONTINUOUSLY EVOLVING

I must be willing to give up what I am in order to become what I will be.

– ALBERT EINSTEIN

Continuously Evolving is voluntarily making steady and incremental progress in developing ourselves. Fortunately, the bedrock assumption of Continuously Evolving is the gains will be incremental. Radical innovation requires significant investment, carries a high degree of risk, and seeks to completely replace the existing. Most of us really don't want to replace ourselves. Here is the premise of this book in a nutshell:

> *Seek to make small but intentional improvements in the direction of your vision and you will Level Up to close the Gap.*

Leveling Up is all about using your strengths to improve your competencies and become *abundant*. You will have *more* of what you need to take you where you want to go.

Continuously Evolving, you voluntarily take yourself out of your comfort zone when it will help you improve your performance.

It can feel daunting to be constantly improving all the time. A significant benefit of the Level Up Method is that using it *reduces* overwhelm, one competency-strength combo at a time.

An effective approach to Continuously Evolving is to focus on three aspects of your life that can yield big returns:

1. your relationships with other people
2. your relationship with time
3. internal reflection

When is the best time to initiate self-development? The answer may surprise you. The best time to begin making things better is when everything is going well. What? Think about it. When stuff needs to be done, you really have no choice but to attend to it. How you do so is up to you (competency-strength combos!), but *what* you do, not so much. When life is wonderful, we get to choose what comes next.

REFINE YOUR RELATIONSHIPS WITH OTHERS

In Chapter 9, Collaborating, we examined how to use our strengths when *building* productive relationships. We now turn our attention to the importance of *maintaining* and *improving* our relationships.

Good relationships. Once you've got 'em, you have to work to keep 'em. Spend some effort preserving them rather than watching them dissolve from neglect.

Make a list of those important to you with whom you are not in regular contact. Find a way to keep in touch with them.

Relationships are strengthened when both parties continue to bring something fresh to the table. Consider which of your strengths are best suited to building relationships. Contrast them with the strengths that can help you refine those relationships. Bringing new strengths into your relationships helps them remain fresh.

During any relationship, as one or both parties change, so too will the relationship. Bringing something into being is one thing, keeping it vital and durable is another.

ASK YOUR CALENDAR TO HONOR YOUR PRIORITIES

Thankfully, here is where we will *not* see a big section on time management. You've heard it all before: goals, plans, timeboxing, etc.

Rather, let's live our lives like Ike, scheduling and attending to what is Important but not Urgent. Let the unimportant and urgent stuff find its own way into our schedules.

CHAPTER 11 - IMPROVING

MAKE TIME FOR INTENTIONAL REFLECTION

Reflecting is thinking about our attitudes and actions in the past, our motives and goals in the present, and how we can improve in the future. Include some time for regular reflection in your life.

This last section in our Continuously Evolving competency gives encouragement to periodically hit the pause button in your life.

Almost everything will work again if you unplug it for a few minutes...including you.

– ANN LAMOTT

Plan some time for regular reflection, a combination of a time-out and me time. One benefit of reflection is the opportunity it provides for voluntary course correction. With pauses to reflect, you can better anticipate forks in the road before you suddenly come upon them at 70 mph.

These final examples show how strengths can enhance our competencies. By examining the personal strengths Appreciation of Beauty and Excellence and Spirituality, along with the two performance strengths Discipline and Intellection, we can improve at Continuously Evolving.

CONTINUOUSLY IMPROVING WITH YOUR PERSONAL STRENGTHS

APPRECIATION OF BEAUTY AND EXCELLENCE

Intentional self-development can be hard work. Thankfully, beyond ourselves lies a whole other world that is ours to admire and aspire to—the world of beauty and excellence in others.

Our strength Appreciation of Beauty and Excellence is the doorway through which we can enter that world.

Use your Appreciation of Beauty and Excellence to help you evolve by more fully appreciating what pleases your senses or you find admirable in others. When you do, your sights will be lifted and your perception of what is possible will soar.

SPIRITUALITY

Some strengths give us a nice *push* to improve. The strengths of Appreciation of Beauty and Excellence and Spirituality are ones we can use to *pull* ourselves up a bit. Those with the strength Spirituality are not limited to improving themselves by what they can find in their own world. They know they are connected to something bigger than themselves and can draw upon it for inspiration to become better.

Use your Spirituality strength to continuously evolve by pulling yourself toward your life's calling, toward your sacred beliefs of divinity, or toward your secular beliefs in humankind. Whatever the nature of your Spirituality strength, it can connect you to the realm beyond our range of human physical experience.

CONTINUOUSLY IMPROVING WITH YOUR PERFORMANCE STRENGTHS

DISCIPLINE

Discipline, the strength without a snooze button on its alarm clock, is a nice one to have when we are Continuously Evolving. After all, "delayed improving" is not what we're after. Discipline is the man with a plan. Discipline likes routine, structure, and doing its part. What is the biggest obstacle most of us face when trying to improve? Getting started, right? Discipline *loves* showing up on time.

When it's time to get serious about developing yourself, engage your Discipline for an assist. Discipline can help you structure your life in a way that optimizes your relationships, uses your time productively, and includes periodic reflection.

INTELLECTION

Intellection, with its capacity for quiet reflection and consideration, is a great strength to help us determine the direction of our self-improvement.

We all know people who overschedule themselves and, as a result, produce a lot of busyness. It seems like their work and their play are always expanding to fill the time available. Unrestrained, they can self-induce "hurry sickness," the stress and anxiety that result from continual feelings of urgency.

Engage your Intellection to put the brakes on that nonsense. What does Intellection do? Intellection *thinks carefully* before initiating action. If you could benefit from better planning and course correcting to help you be Continuously Evolving, engage Intellection to help you think things through.

PART III

THE NEXT VERSION OF YOU
You Are Ready

> *The beginning is always today.*
>
> – MARY SHELLEY

You are now prepared to use the Level Up concepts to take yourself on a journey. Your destination: the next happier, more fulfilled version of you. On your voyage, you will occasionally be out of your comfort zone. To achieve what you desire, you will have to do some things differently. It will take a while to get used to your new habits. Some uneasiness is natural when consciously improving ourselves. Remember, growth and comfort cannot co-exist.

> **You can either step forward into growth, or backwards into security.**
>
> – ABRAHAM MASLOW

It won't be easy. Neither will it be terribly hard; 80 percent effort will be plenty.

As you test competency-strength combos on things you want to do in your life, you will have the sensation you are moving. You will become unstuck! You will become more optimistic and enthusiastic. And your self-belief will soar.

Now is when you give yourself permission to cease doing anything that isn't moving you toward a happier, more fulfilled you.

For a quick start, visualize a few things you would like to do more of and some you would prefer to do less of. The simple act of imagining a little better version of you will put you in a positive place.

Go for a few small wins early. Nothing provides momentum and hope like achieving something. Start with Goldilocks efforts: not too hard, but not too easy.

CHOOSE & USE

Every time you choose and use a competency-strength combination, you will experience a little lift and feel encouraged to repeat the experience.

PART III - THE NEXT VERSION OF YOU

ONE AT A TIME, PLEASE...

Each of us has the potential to improve in so many ways. But dedicate yourself to no more than three, one at a time. Focus on a small handful of things and address them in as few steps as possible.

For an impressive example of simplifying the incomprehensible, ponder NASA's mission to land men on the moon and safely return them. The challenge was issued in 1961 by JFK.

This was going to be an incredibly complex task. But rather than starting with the complicated, they went the other direction, toward simplification, and asked, "To win this war, what is the fewest number of battles we need to win?"

They used this narrowing process to arrive at:

> Propulsion, Navigation, Life Support

Of course, there is no comparison between the challenges NASA faced and the ones we deal with in our lives. Still, fewer is usually better. The fewer steps from your bed to the bathroom, the fewer miles in your commute, the fewer clubs you need to get around the golf course, and—unless you are an entertainer—the fewer people you must please. Likewise, the fewer improvements we need to be happier, the more likely we are to succeed. Just like a machine, fewer moving parts = less potential for breakdown.

You already have everything you need to become a happier you—your potential to live a more fulfilling life, your natural strengths, and your competencies. With these, your efforts will become less erratic and more productive. As your progress becomes smoother, your confidence will rise. Satisfaction, and the sense that you are thriving, will follow.

You don't need the concentration of a jeweler to make this work for you. As long as you approach it with intention and commitment, you will be fine.

Occasionally, take some shots that are a stretch for you. When you know doing so will not cause any collateral damage, go for it. That's how you grow. Surprise yourself.

Next up, in our final chapter, is a simple and straightforward approach you can use to elevate your life.

CHAPTER 12

YOUR PERSONAL DEVELOPMENT PLAN

USE YOUR COMPETENCY-STRENGTH COMBOS TO CLOSE THE GAP

Remember the Gap, the difference between where we are going and where we want to go in our lives?

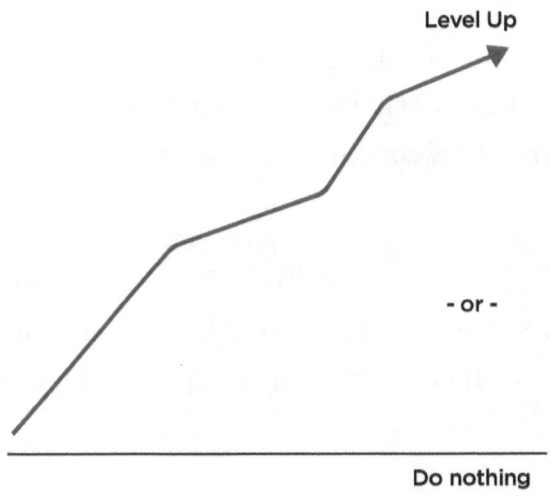

Have you ever been told to think outside the box? Annoying, wasn't it? Most of what is outside the box is *impossible.* A more useful, and agreeable, concept is "think *inside* the Gap." Use the mental picture of the Gap you want to fill to focus on what is *possible.*

Ways to think *in* the Gap:

> Where am I now?
> Where do I want to go?
> When do I want to arrive?
> What do I need to improve?
> What can I do first to get underway?

Think of a small improvement you would like to make for yourself.

MAYBE TRY THIS...

Sometimes we are unable to express ourselves accurately. To help me when I get stuck writing, I put three sets of labels on the lower frame of my computer screen:

BE USEFUL	INSPIRE	BE BRIEF
BE INTERESTING	GIVE HOPE	BE BOLD
BE ENTERTAINING	ENCOURAGE	BE CLEAR

A quick glance at them never fails to give me an idea of what to do next.

■

To help you find the right combo to try first, select the competency *category* and the strength *set* that feel like logical starting places. Using our Competency-Strength Grid below, begin by considering the possible combos within just one of the 25 squares.

For a quick reference to the strengths in each set and the competencies in each category, see the APPENDIX.

COMPETENCY-STRENGTH GRID

Use your Strengths	to improve your **Competencies**				
	PLANNING	CHANGING	COLLAB-ORATING	ACCOM-PLISHING	IMPROVING
THINKING	X	X	X	X	X
CONNECTING	X	X	X	X	X
ENABLING	X	X	X	X	X
PERFORMING	X	X	X	X	X
BELIEVING	X	X	X	X	X

Consider which of your combos in a square could help you do something. Nothing here? How about another square, one with the same category of competency but a different set of strength?

Play with this a bit until you identify a square with categories that feel natural to you.

Are you thinking there are a lot of possible competency-strength combos? There are indeed—58 strengths and 17 competencies make for 986 different competency-strength combinations. If there is something that cannot be addressed with one of these, I have yet to discover it.

Thankfully, we will have to consider but a few to make progress on any specific issue. In most cases, there may be 1-3 competencies that will be useful, and 1-5 of our signature strengths that could support them.

Approach making progress with your competency-strength combo as you would a safe with a two-dial combination lock. The first number, the competency, is between 1 and 3. The second number, the signature strength you will apply, is between 1 and 5. If there was something you really wanted in a safe and there were only 15 combinations, would you try them? Of course, you would. A few turns of the wheels and, eventually, open sesame!

CHAPTER 12 - YOUR PERSONAL DEVELOPMENT PLAN

PSST...

Want to know the powerful secret to using your strengths to improve your competencies? It's *practice*.

That's it. If you practice them, they will come. If you don't? Well, you know...

Practice using your competency-strengths combos to rehearse your future and decrease the distance between you and your potential.

Finally, we have a template, the Five Steps to a Better You, you can use to practice thriving in new ways.

5 STEPS TO A BETTER YOU
INCREASE HAPPINESS AND SENSE OF THRIVING

1. To be better at:

_____

2. I will first work on this:

_____

3. I will try to accomplish it by using these combos:

<u>Competency</u>   supported by   <u>Strength</u>

a.   —

b.   —

c.   —

4. The combination that felt most natural was:

_____ — _____

5. I will try to use this to:

_____

CHAPTER 12 - YOUR PERSONAL DEVELOPMENT PLAN

TIME TO CELEBRATE!

Congratulations are in order. You stuck with this and learned how to use competencies to channel your unique strengths and take your life to the next level.

For a reminder of how far you've come, take a moment to revisit the Table of Contents. There is now a lot more of you—to think, to change, to collaborate and to make forward progress in your life.

I hope *Level Up* has given you some new energy and optimism with which to continue your expedition toward a happier, more fulfilled you.

Bon voyage!

DID YOU...

...enjoy reading *Level Up*? If so, the best way to thank an author is to leave a review on Amazon and share your experience with others.

Thank you kindly,
Mike

ABOUT THE AUTHOR

Michael is fortunate to have over 20 years' Leadership experience in a variety of organizations, such as Scouting America, the Air Force Reserves, The Boys & Girls Clubs, and engineering and financial services companies. As a shirt sleeve team leader, he has helped many others understand and reach their potential.

Utilizing his US-EU dual citizenship, he is also an avid world traveler, having visited over 70 countries, which has provided him an appreciation for the similarities and differences of others.

As an author, he inspires others to reach their potential and live their best lives. *Level Up Your Happiness* is his second book. Today, Mike and his wife, and too many dogs, live in Scottsdale, Arizona.

For more information about Michael, please visit him at www.linkedin.com/in/michael-oster/

APPENDIX

The 5 Sets of Strengths

and

The 5 Categories of Competencies

THE 5 SETS OF STRENGTHS
HOLDING THE 58 UNIQUE STRENGTHS

1. **Thinking:** *Increase your Wisdom*

    with Personal Strengths–from VIA

    Creativity
    Curiosity
    Judgement
    Love of Learning
    Perspective

    with Performance Strengths–from Gallup

    Analytical
    Context
    Futuristic
    Ideation
    Input
    Intellection
    Learner
    Strategic

2. **Connecting:** *Engage with People and Support Them*

    with Personal Strengths–from VIA

    Fairness
    Honesty
    Love
    Social Intelligence
    Teamwork

    with Performance Strengths–from Gallup

    Empathy
    Harmony
    Includer
    Individualization
    Positivity
    Relator

APPENDIX

3   **Enabling**: *Have a Positive Effect on People*

with Personal Strengths–from VIA

Forgiveness	Kindness
Humility	Humor
Leadership	

with Performance Strengths–from Gallup

Communication	Significance
Developer	Woo
Self-Assurance	

4   **Performing**: *Do Your Best*

with Personal Strengths–from VIA

Bravery	Self-Regulation
Perseverance	Zest
Prudence	

with Performance Strengths–from Gallup

Achiever	Deliberative
Activator	Discipline
Adaptability	Focus
Arranger	Maximizer
Command	Responsibility
Competition	Restorative
Consistency	

5   **Believing:** *Live Your Values*

   with Personal Strengths–from VIA

   Appreciation of Beauty and Excellence
   Gratitude   Spirituality
   Hope

   with Performance Strengths–from Gallup

   Belief   Connectedness

APPENDIX

THE 5 CATEGORIES OF COMPETENCIES
HOLDING THE 17 UNIQUE COMPETENCIES

1. **Planning:** *Have the Will and Intention to Do Something*
   Creating Vision
   Making Decisions
   Developing Plans

2. **Changing:** *Accept What's Next*
   Tolerating
   Risk
   Negotiating
   Communicating Clearly

3. **Collaborating:** *Work with Others on Common Goals*
   Building Productive Relationships
   Inspiring Others
   Developing Others
   Influencing Others
   Leading Teams
   Managing Conflict

4. **Accomplishing:** *Finish What You Start*
   Taking Initiative
   Executing Efficiently

5. **Improving:** *Practice Self-Awareness and Self-Care*
   Continually Learning
   Acting Professionally
   Continuously Evolving

INDEX

References to Strengths

PERSONAL STRENGTHS*

Appreciation of Beauty and Excellence 80, 204
Bravery 66, 129
Creativity 37, 113
Curiosity 37, 193
Fairness 46, 169
Forgiveness 56, 150
Gratitude 82, 151
Honesty 47, 145
Hope 82, 179
Humility 57, 152
Humor 58, 139
Judgement 38, 108
Kindness 58, 157
Leadership 59, 180
Love 48, 146
Love of Learning 38, 194
Perseverance 68, 134
Perspective 39, 102
Prudence 68, 109
Self-Regulation 69, 198
Social Intelligence 48, 161
Spirituality 83, 204
Teamwork 49, 164
Zest 70, 183

* from the VIA Institute

PERFORMANCE STRENGTHS**

Achiever 70, 184
Activator 71, 181
Adaptability 72, 129
Analytical 40, 109
Arranger 72, 103, 165
Belief 84, 199
Command 73, 140
Communication 60, 134, 170
Competition 73, 165
Connectedness 85, 152
Consistency 74, 154
Context 40, 196
Deliberative 74, 184
Developer 60
Discipline 75, 205
Empathy 50, 141
Focus 75, 185
Futuristic 41, 103, 196
Harmony 50, 147
Ideation 41, 110
Includer 51, 153
Individualization 51, 158, 171
Input 42, 113
Intellection 42, 206
Learner 43, 195
Maximizer 76, 159
Positivity 52, 130
Relator 52, 147
Responsibility 76, 185
Restorative 77, 181
Self-Assurance 61, 135
Significance 62, 162
Strategic 44, 114
Woo: "Winning Others Over" 62, 199

**from Gallup, Inc.

www.ingramcontent.com/pod-product-compliance
Lightning Source LLC
Chambersburg PA
CBHW030548080526
44585CB00012B/306